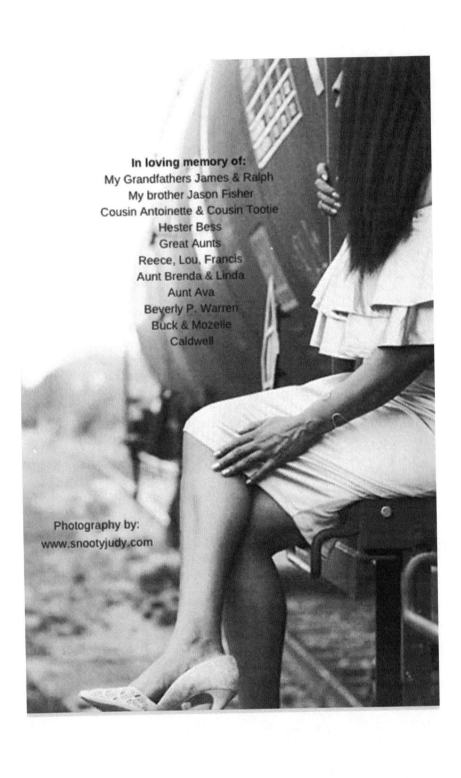

In loving memory of:
My Grandfathers James & Ralph
My brother Jason Fisher
Cousin Antoinette & Cousin Tootie
Hester Bess
Great Aunts
Reece, Lou, Francis
Aunt Brenda & Linda
Aunt Ava
Beverly P. Warren
Buck & Mozelie
Caldwell

Photography by:
www.snootyjudy.com

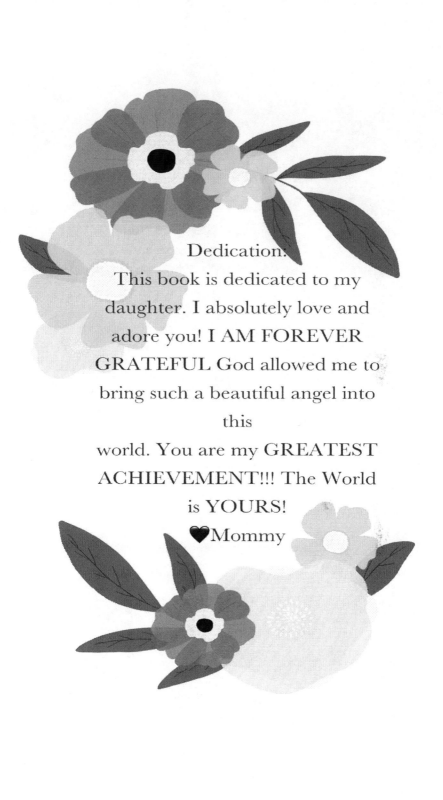

Dedication:
This book is dedicated to my
daughter. I absolutely love and
adore you! I AM FOREVER
GRATEFUL God allowed me to
bring such a beautiful angel into
this
world. You are my GREATEST
ACHIEVEMENT!!! The World
is YOURS!
♥Mommy

**Flight Fight Freeze**
Experiencers of trauma and abuse do not
speak up immediately. Often many
unexposed to trauma find this hard to believe.
Regardless of age, the brain can hold
information until it's ready to be released.
The flight mechanism comes into play when it
is in the best favor of the victim or targeted
person to flee from trauma or situations going
on.
The fight can occur at any time the trauma or
abuse is voiced. Anyone that triggers,
questions period, coerces silence or urges
the victim to forgive without hearing them can
become an enemy.
The freezing stage can be extensive. Victims
bury occurrences in the back of their minds,
and can even be in proximity to those
responsible for the trauma. Mentally the
trauma can be difficult to deal with, it's easier
for some to continue family connections with
relatives that may pridefully abandon them
once they vocalize their experience(s).

Photography By
Tshombie Smith

## About Author

Michelle Washington is a native of Winston-Salem, North Carolina, and a mother that enjoys creating all things beautiful!

She graduated from Reynolds High School. The Upward Bound Pre-College program at Winston-Salem State University played a humongous part in her educational development as a teen.

The celebrity cosmetologist earned her cosmetology license at Leon's Beauty School in Greensboro, N.C.

A huge believer that "your gifts will make room for you," Michelle's God-given gifts successfully established opportunities in her city to cultivate the first Flag Ministry and acceptance of the honorable invite to style hair for the National Black Theater Festival Fashion Show at her favorite places to give back to; the church and community.

Raised in a wholesome Christian home, Childhood Sexual Trauma became her reality once marriage landed her in a blended family at the age of 6.

Encounters with women throughout life, silently desiring to heal from childhood trauma; unanimously stating "I never told anyone; no one would believe me," sounded familiar to Michelle.

The journey to healing herself and others began once the effects of childhood sexual trauma impacted her adulthood and family bonds.

Journaling when no one would listen shaped her first book based on true life experiences among many books to come!

Maturity called her to author books that boldly snatch back those large area rugs in families that reveal decades of mountain-high secrets and curses nationwide that affect the lives of the abused!

For information about bulk purchases, speaking engagements and to book one on one healing sessions please contact the author at

ladylikechurchgirl2023@gmail.com

Social Media  Platforms

Instagram: @ladylikechurchgirl

Facebook: Llcg Book

Youtube: Ladylike ChurchgirlISBN:

(Paperback)

ISBN:

(Digital)

Printed in the United States of America

# Disclaimer

Unless otherwise stated, to protect the privacy of certain individuals the names have been changed to fictitious names in the publication.

Names of friends dear to the author were used for the sole purpose of name substitutes and inclusion.

Either the author or publisher shall be held liable or responsible for any loss or damage allegedly arising from any suggestion or information contained in this book.

# LadyLike

# CHURCH GIRL

Michelle Washington

# TABLE OF CONTENTS

# Introduction

April 2, 1974, at 12:47 a.m., a child was born to a virgin. Undoubtedly my 17-year-old mother and father had a fun Fourth of July Weekend in 1973. What a big decision at such a young age to become parents!!

Knowing most teen parents are unhappy to conceive so young, I'm positive a discussion of what they would do came up.

Babies feel this rejection in the womb. On Earth, they someday realize the spirit has attached itself to them. As if people could see their energy, they continuously fall into traps with those who benefit from signs of weakness. Undergoing rejection has given me the strength to share my experience.

# Charm School

My grandmother Nan assisted with raising me.  Nan's mother, my Great Grandma Booker, raised her and her twelve children Christian, so naturally, Nan instilled those same values in my momma and her oldest and middle girls, Zaria and India. They passed the same traditions down to their children.

We lived in the "projects" with neighbors we cared for like family, and I loved it. There was always lots of laughter and countless children at our family together. On Saturdays, Sunday dinner would simmer. After service, the family would meet at Nan's, where soul food and laughter filled the air. Momma and Aunt Z randomly belted out their favorite parts of songs from the service. India unlike her two sisters was not a big churchgoer Saturday night while we rested supporting her husband who played the guitar professionally was her mood.

It wasn't a meal if Cornbread or Biscuits wasn't present.

The newspaper was spread out on the floor for the kids to sit on while adults sat at the table in the kitchen.

Momma and her sisters would sometimes argue over the last piece of bread. Nan was indeed the Queen of her house and our backbone.

Life was sweet and so much fun. Momma and Nan were like 16 superstars to me. I absorbed everything they did, were doing, wearing, and even feeling. Poised, proper, and dignified, the beautiful, independent Matriarch of our family involuntarily was my mom, too, since my momma was a teen. Humble and without an announcement, Nan broke many color barriers and was named among the 1st black waitresses to serve on the "whites only" side at Woolworth Downtown Winston-Salem, North Carolina. The beauty was later hired at Thalhimer's Fashion Fair Cosmetics counter and the first face to greet customers that entered the Fourth Street entrance of the store Downtown. Women from the community loved to purchase makeup and skincare products from her; it was the Mac Makeup of the '70s! Nan was about her Father's business when she wasn't working and had a way of doing things.

Nan exuded class and set very high standards and could've opened a charm school with all her "dos and don'ts" for young ladies. As far as she was concerned, young ladies did not whistle or play cards, especially on Sundays! Red polish, red lipstick, and anklets were forbidden. I never saw it on the lips of Nan or momma.

On New Year's Day, Nan gave an annual dinner for her and all of her sisters. Of course, I was the only child present. The majority of Nan's sister's children were my great cousins although some of us were close in age. The fellowship was beautiful. They caught up at the table for hours. Eventually, Aunt India transformed the New Year's Day dinner into a family dinner; and a game of Pokémon. I watched everyone pull out tons of pennies and prepare to play, wondering if we couldn't play cards, what they were doing playing this board game decorated with playing cards. I only knew how to play "Go Fish" and Uno. Gambling on Sundays was a BIG "no no!"

Nan was an early riser. The smell of coffee filled the air when I opened my eyes. Sunday, was the day Nan said God wanted us to rest. No heavy labor was done, not even a load of laundry, but cooking was permitted, although the majority was done Saturday. Nan prepared a big breakfast with sausage, grits, and toast. On other days she kept it simple. Some mornings Special K (my favorite) Total or Cornflakes cereal with banana slices were on the menu. Grapefruit lightly dusted with sugar was constantly refreshing in the summer months. Nan cut it for me so well that my spoon scooped the triangular pieces out effortlessly!

In the Mornings the weather was suitable; we sat on the porch in the gliding chair swing. Only older people were up; I'd be in pajamas. The Black-owned Milk Truck Company came through. Some Saturday evenings, after it cooled off, we would return to a completely different and adults walking, talking, and socializing. Aside from playing with my next-door neighbor, whom I called my 'first best friend," Iyana, I was always welcome to play in the yard or in-ear and eyeshot of Nan with three of my little girlfriends that lived in the row of apartments across the street Cherry who visited her grandmother Ms. Marie often, Karin and Shmook whose mom favored my Aunt Z. I kind of get why Nan tried to protect me because one of the times I did go inside a neighbor's house with a friend we entered the room while her aunt recovering from surgery was showing the wound to my friend mom. Seeing it made my stomach weak; I wish we had knocked before we entered.

# Eyes Wide Shut

Amos, momma's daddy, was employed at RJ Reynolds Tobacco which was a big to-do in my city! He moved back home with his momma, my great grandma Dessie when he and Nan's marriage failed.

I love that momma stayed connected to her father's family despite her parent's breakup. Grandma Dessie babysat me while she worked. I couldn't speak but was aware momma had left and the morning routine. I'd be at the kitchen table, possibly finishing or having breakfast. Like clockwork Uncle Chic, my granddaddy's brother, would enter the kitchen and make Sanka Instant coffee every morning. My granddaddy was not functioning on a regular frequency. Sleeping was how he spent his time. That was fine with me. At least I had access to him!

There was a magnetic pull to go downstairs. Little ole me would go down to the dim and chilly basement to find granddaddy sleeping peacefully. He was chocolate, slim, and handsome, lying down as if he barely made it in the door. I wish his eyes were open. I bet they were brown. Even knowing the sound of his voice would have been excellent.

Thankfully I heard the good things from Aunt India; they were close. My granddaddy taught her how to fight. There had to be a time he was a decent man if he made time to teach his daughter how to protect herself. So when others labeled him an alcoholic, I questioned the root of what made him drink so heavily he slept the days away.

I decided to visualize one peaceful time Nan spoke about their courtship. She and my grandfather were hanging out back at his mother's in the grass on a blanket and got a glimpse of her dad leaving out the back door of a house in view. "Amos, there goes my daddy," she said. "That man is at that house all the time," my grandfather responded to her dismay. Although the conversation made me aware of how my great-grandfather got down, I can imagine it was a warm day, and they were young and happy!

The first time I witnessed him and Nan in the same radius was the last time I saw my granddaddy. He was casket sharp, eyes wide shut in his coffin. Alive in his presence, he couldn't see me, consumed with his issues. Until we met again, I hope during his life review in Heaven, he saw me by his side.

Nan's only choice was to make drastic decisions to protect herself and her girls from him during his drunkenness. I heard he was so out of control a pot of scolding hot water awaited him during their last encounter.

I understood something had transpired. Jim Crow laws ran the south, and brown skin was a target. I loved my granddaddy and wished things turned out differently for his life! I'm grateful momma allowed me to spend time with this part of my village; it gave me a glimpse into my granddaddy's side of the family.

# Momma, You Know I Love You

Momma was the younger version of Nan and the youngest of her sisters, Zaria and India.

The Bible on her dresser held a photo of the newspaper article photo in Bell-bottoms jeans and a mid-drift shirt capturing her in beautiful African braids with one beaded braid adorning her forehead. This photo made me so proud I thought it was so lovely a newspaper photographer captured her essence for an unplanned debut in the City of Winston!

Momma cared well for me as she did for herself. I felt very girly in my outfits and hairstyles. Saturday nights, I got my hair shampooed and prepped for the hard press momma would give me Sunday morning. During my first salon visit with momma, I received a hair chemical called Vigoroll. I adored getting pretty!

Let momma's sisters Zaria and India tell it; momma was going to wash the skin off me. She bathed me so much.

Nothing held her down.

After birthing me, she secured a neighborhood sitter, Mrs. Green, to keep me while working at the hospital. I was so young I couldn't speak, but my visual perception was sharp. Her salt and pepper hairstyle was similar to Florida Evans; all I remember was the smiles she gave me. I got there early, so the lights were off except in the kitchen, where a Honey Combs cereal box sat on the table. Her son eventually entered the kitchen for breakfast, and I would stare as he chattered with baby me. The fact I was a small child did not negate the fact I recognized he was easy on the eyes with a happy demeanor like his mom.

Undefined by her circumstances, Momma got a new gig in the retail loan department at Wachovia. That was a big deal. Looking very professional in her signature mushroom hairstyle that perfectly framed her face and complemented the rich, timeless clothing, she could drive like she raced cars for a living! On days we ran late, momma went fast, took shortcuts, and had no problem pulling up in reverse to the sitters.

Weekends we're exciting. Momma did laundry in the morning. During the spin cycle, momma would sit on the washing machine, holding me as it moved all over the floor; we laughed so hard Nan would've had a fit if she knew!!!!

After the chores were complete, we hung out. The first stops were the farmers market for her Sunday stockings and the "Meat House." Aunt Z rode with us sometimes. Then the fun began at the shopping center!! Lunch at Sally's Hotdogs & pizza was our favorite!!! The day ended earlier when momma and Aunt Z had choir rehearsal. I knew every song the young adult choir sang.

When the choir members weren't listening, the choir director yelled at them with his hand on his hip like someone's mother, and his long process curls shook! He joked with them a lot too. Some spoke of clubs they would go to later that night after choir rehearsal.

Momma would be ready to go as soon as rehearsal ended, Aunt Z liked to socialize. On one occasion, momma told Aunt Z "let's go," countless times and Aunt Z kept chatting; I was shocked when momma cranked the car and left her in the parking lot. As soon as we arrived home, we could barely get out of the car; Nan was at the door and mandated that momma go right back and get her. My cousins Ryan and Chance probably wondered what took their mom so long to return. There was still a group gathered when we returned to pick her up. I couldn't believe momma had left her sister!

As a kid, you don't say much, but what I took in was molding me.

# Sweetest Thing

Sunday after dinner, during all the excitement and chatter of momma and her sisters, I'd dash up that walkway on Sundays to my dad's momma, Grandma Maury's house. Grandma Maury said I'd come over without permission and sit in Coolie room until he arrived home. When Nan called out for me, she would let her know I was there.

The experience was always eventful; Coolie was one of five, so all my cousins would be there after church. I wanted to be a part; I invited myself! I liked that they gave me the nickname Mimi and how Grandma squeezed me into a hug and called me "baby," no money could top that! The love and affection she exuded when "I came around" was contagious!

The experience was always eventful; my dad was one of five, so all my cousins would be there after church. I wanted to be a part; I invited myself! I liked that they gave me the nickname Mimi!

Grandma Maury was notorious for cooking large meals for her kids and their family. The house felt like home as the door swung open and shut as everyone went about when "I visited."

Back in the day, Grandma went to beauty school; she naturally was a caregiver without schooling. She cooked at restaurants; the family laughed at rumors the men came to watch grandma stir the grits. Lol! Her home was kept spotless. She had a gift for cleaning and did it professionally at the hospital.

Fashion was big on my dad's side. I was amused when I'd catch her in jeans and a leather coat. With no shame in her game, "PRAISE THE LORD " is how she answered the phone. Christian TV was always on in her room. Scriptures taped to the walls were visible as you brushed your teeth or stood at the kitchen sink. PTL's "Praise the Lord " was her favorite network. The Network's waterpark had my eye's attention; as my nose took in the aroma of incense coming from under the crack of Uncle Miles' door beside her room. She loved the church; I'm a witness to her love for God and her spirit of giving.

One Christmas, Grandma had a birthday cake with HAPPY BIRTHDAY on it, and I asked whose birthday it was "it's Jesus' birthday, baby." she responded, making it easier to face the observers who seemingly knew whose birthday it was. Nan, momma, and I went to church, and I got baptized. Christmas celebrated at Nan's was beautiful. She even did a skit, "Silent Night Holy Night for church, but I had never heard of Jesus' birthday till that day; I only knew God. Grandma, on the other hand, grandly recognized the guest of honor at dinner! That day after singing Happy Birthday to Jesus while eating cake from my favorite bakery, I learned it wasn't just about gifts and that the white man with the long hair in the clouds that hung in her living room was Our Savior and God's son.

# My Twin

Ralph Fisher, my dad's father, and I look like twins! His face is mine; I look more like him than all of his children. His birthday was three days after my birthday!

I have been told awesome things about him by everyone. He took great pride in himself and his surroundings. He was very organized and enjoyed deep cleaning.

I know my creative edge comes from him. Home Improvement and decor are passions that ran through his blood.

Unfortunately, he passed right before I was born in a car accident at 34 years of age, headed to Greensboro, North Carolina. In the '70s, drinking on the weekend after working hard all week was normal. Some drank so often lives were affected by it.

My grandfather was a great provider. He offered home improvement services in and out of state. The gifts he contributed to society manifest to in his children's lives financially and blessed them.

Alcoholism and addiction, along with other traits absorbed into the bloodline.

# One Love

My father, who I called "COOLIE," carried himself with the utmost dignity, immaculately styled while doing so! Unfortunately, he and his father did not always see eye to eye.

Handsome and new in the projects, not only did he meet my momma, but he made new friends there, in the surrounding community and public school system. Gleaming and modeling the adults he encountered. Coolie gave respect and high regard to his friends' fathers pursuing healthy relationships with their developing sons. The backgrounds of those he associated with were so positive he became an Omega man while majoring in Early Childhood Development at WSSU.

The ladies loved him PERIOD! Mama told me how she would look out the window as he walked women "friends" up the sidewalk into grandma's front door.

Tennis was his sport of choice. Painting and interior decorating were natural gifts. His talents could've taken him anywhere, but like many, he preferred a full-time job and considered the skills, hobbies, and things he made time for on the side.

Our project house was situated at the entrance of that walkway leading to Coolie's house. My room had the best views, they didn't see invisible me, but I saw my dad's family come and go up the long walkway that led to his house.

I couldn't imagine my daughter/grandchild/niece a rock throw away and not visiting her. Still, my dad's family, who profusely loved Jesus, did! They formally invited church members and I was a popup. Pop-ups were cool and great family perks, but I wanted the "full package" family membership beyond food and church services.

The proximity of our houses allotted me glimpses of his White Volkswagen Bug, sometimes parked right in front of our house. Unbothered, I took what I could get, settling with the stimulation that arose from the sight of his car parked. No knock at the front door, his car, in my small eyes, represented him, and stood in proxy of him. Maybe the man just parked in the space available although hiding the car like he hid made more sense. The visibility of the vehicle didn't faze him, his brain didn't register how parking in such proximity while being absent in your daughter's confused me. Knowing Coolie was home comforted me, although the Early Childhood Development major wasn't checking for me.

Smashing my face on the window screen to see if his car was parked further up the street was customary when his car wasn't parked out front. I'd stare to no avail, powerless that I could never catch the smooth operator pull up. The car was as close to him as I could get, but he found time to date, post up at parties, and attend college homecomings.

It was obvious Coolie communicated well with women despite omitting to communicate with his offspring. The man was girl crazy!

Coolie moved into his place without telling me. Call me crazy, but anytime I was in the car, I peered out the windows and effortlessly spotted white Volkswagen Bugs in hopes it was him. I could tell by the back window. His VW had a rainbow sticker stuck to the rear windshield. It was never him, I doubt Momma would've pulled over if I spotted him. Just seeing him would've been nice. She didn't care I longed to see him. No one had asked her about her thoughts growing up, I couldn't blame her.

Coolie rocked Stan Smith Adidas. The Green and white Stan Smith Adidas sneakers caught my attention when I saw them on someone's feet, I'd think of him.

Miraculously my 5th birthday is my fondest memory. On this day my Coolie and I went shopping before my party. I selected Wonder Woman underoos and trendy 70's Buster Brown Shoes like the kids at school had. After shopping, we made several stops, and my dad introduced me to his friends. We even stopped by a female friend's condo. I looked out the window as we parked at the manicured lawn and tennis courts. The neighborhood impressed me.

Coolie brought me back to "The Circle before the party was about to start. "Aunt Z" hosted the party in her backyard. This part of the neighborhood was less traveled and offered more privacy than Nan's.

The party was music-themed with white table clothes; I peeked at the Dewey's box, which contained a white cake with white icing. Miniature black records were all over the top with candles.

Aunt Z two sons, Ryan and Chance, were there. They were like my brothers, although we were cousins. I could explore more at their place. I was at her house so much, the majority of the guest were her neighbors and her friend's children.

Aunt India and her family hadn't arrived. The party wasn't complete without Uncle Ricardo, Tim, and Tamonica's arrival. The party hadn't even started, but the day was already unforgettable. Thanks to "My Coolie" I will never forget that day.

# The Trinity

Good and bad, ups and downs, I am them; they are me. I had the potential to become or not to become good or bad and option to avoid or experience the ups and downs of my forefathers. At stages in my life, I too may select from the family bowl of fruit that looked delicious only discover I digested poison.

The family traits passed to me from my parents with a taste of EXODUS 34:7 that mentions, "But He will not leave the guilty unpunished, bringing the consequences of the fathers' wrongdoing on the children and grandchildren to the third and fourth generation," were enough to make a newborn want crawl back in the womb.

# Proverb 22:6

Train up a child in the way he should go: and when he is old, he will not depart from it.

The church is where many church girls and boys were exposed to adults conversing that were incognizant of the effects of the words they spoke and language used in the presence of children. I couldn't give feedback, but I became a great listener to adults' conversation. Getting the gossip aka tea was easy! Nan loved chatting on the phone and despite her attempts to whisper I still got an ear full. Nan got it in but um, Aunt Z conversations were JUICIER; I had a front row seat to her conversations laying right beside her bed when she thought I was looking at television or asleep. Tea was being served and spilt everywhere; church parking lot tea, after-church tea, dinner tea, and telephone tea. Then there was the Young Adult choir tea. Lives of the saints was pretty interesting outside of the four walls.

Not only was I an only child but I was the only granddaughter and niece before my younger cousin Tamonica was born, I tagged along everywhere the ladies in my family went; momma always drove.

During Christmas it was so hard to believe in Santa because I went Christmas shopping with momma and my aunties. I saw the gifts Aunt Z and India purchased for Ryan, Chance and Tim. I got yelled at for telling them about a few gifts to expect.

# Come Sunday

Sunday was the highlight of my week, the fear scriptures instilled in me. I saw choir members and Bible Study attendees transform incredibly! It was a fashion show! Everyone looked well-rested, smiling as they said "Good morning" in good English. The entire congregation looked and smelled rich! Every hair on females was in place, and the males had a fresh cut! There were hundreds of hairstyles to watch.

Nan was in leadership, so when I went to church with her, we were up with the chickens to eat and get dressed before the church van arrived. I noticed the driver smoking along with others and the ashtray full of cigarette butts. I thought the van belonged to God, so I was confused about why ashtrays were in the church van, anyway? Kids didn't understand churches purchased the vans from a dealership. We had to believe whatever adults said but ignore the contradictions.

The friendly van driver parked at the front door. Everyone waited while he opened the doors and placed a wooden two-step stoop at the lip of the van door for a safe exit.

Nan and I headed straight to the finance office where the big wigs hung out, and she hung up our coats and socialized until Sunday school started at 9:45 am. Not lugging around a heavy coat allow me to freely sport my church outfits with no interference. I was in the Primary Department. Mrs. Johnson was my 1st grade Sunday school teacher, and she was my favorite!

Her tone was very proper matching all the class she exuded with her pretty chocolate skin. The room had small fold-up chairs with large windows parents peered in at the end of class. Each class was age-based; we transitioned to a new teacher in the fall, just like the public school system.

When Sunday school was over I could locate Nan across the hall in the Sunday school office. Nan eventually stopped waiting for me; the gesture made me feel like a big girl roaming the busy church halls after Sunday school classes were over. Fresh faces were arriving for the 11 am service. The vending machine area was active, but I wasn't allowed to eat snacks that early. Momma sometimes got snacks and a soda when service was over.

Momma slept in some Sunday mornings and would arrive as class was released and her purse would be loaded with candy for service; we did not eat the peppermint candy they passed around in church, I wasn't snooty, however the site of that enormous zip lock bag the older saints shared with the assorted "unwrapped" candy stuck together made me turn my nose up.

Sunday's momma had to sing; the lady's lounge was our first stop. It was cute with a sizable wall-to-wall mirror and these bad red puffy pleather, possibly leather couches. The bathroom stalls were in the secondary room of the lounge.

We'd sit in the lounge; space women would primp and comb hair. It was very smoky. "Shut that door," was yelled periodically to keep smoke from traveling in the hallway. Women made you aware of fallen slip lines and told tissue on the bottom of your shoe as you exited.

The scent of Holly Farm's fried chicken and everything Merita Bakery baked lit up our nostrils during the church service; it made me so hungry! Nan cooked every Sunday, but I had Holly Farms Chicken whenever the youth choir had to sing after church.

Monday, things went back to normal, and before you knew it, it would be Sunday again. The Holidays made me the happiest because I loved when my momma took a week off work!

# A Man Appeared

My gorgeous mom snagged a guy named Evan with me in her belly to give you an idea of how extensive her beauty was and most likely why Coolie wasn't stopping by, but anyway, these two met while working at the hospital he has been around since I can remember.

Evan grew up in a home off Sherman with his parents and siblings. When he came over, they hung out in momma's room as any young couple word when parents weren't around. Aunt India complained     about them being in the room because Nan had a fit when she chatted with Uncle Ricardo from her bedroom window. She never would've allowed them to be alone when she lived there!

I accompanied them out sometimes when Nan was at work. The three of us shared the front seat momma sat me beside the door; she sat in the middle beside him in the Dukes of Hazard-looking car. The seatbelt law did not exist, but subconsciously, I think that was my first time feeling rejected.

My momma reminded me of the cartoon characters I watched with red hearts that popped into their eyes when they fell in love. Momma and I still had fun during the day, and she reserved time for her man at night. I enjoyed watching her get ready for the dates. She was all that, and her hair was so thick and pretty. The room would be spotless, her outfit laid out on her bed. While she soaked in the tub, I liked to push the button on her Polaroid Camera that sat on her dresser with her Bible that held the newspaper article she featured in with her intricate braids. I wasn't in her way, and she never dismissed me as I stayed on her heels as she dressed. I can honestly say she was happy as ever! They even traveled.

When he got his first apartment, Momma did a pop-up! I remember it being late, and I could tell she was upset, holding my hand tight the whole time so I could keep up as she walked fast. An exchange of words took place with my mom doing the exchanging mostly. Wonder what he did to make her so upset?

# Going to the Chapel

Momma was born in August and chose to be an August bride. Not sure when he proposed, but I was six when she married. The wedding took place in the chapel of the church Evan attended. Momma looked beautiful in a white gown with faint pink flowers and baby breath adorned in her up do.

A small reception was held at Aunt India's. She and Uncle Ricardo met at 15, married young, and were thick as thieves. My auntie wasn't to be played with and kept me on my toes and teased me at times because I was fearful of dogs and she laughed at the fact.

Our residence changed to the other side of town to Salem Woods, a predominantly white middle-class neighborhood. The brick house was spacious with dark green trim and shutters! It had four entrances! We usually entered the side door to the den, my favorite room, because the accent brick wall had a built-in fireplace with a wall-to-wall brick slab for seating and decor; and the perfect place to lay down in front of fireplace.

The laundry room and kitchen were adjoined to the den and both rooms had entry and exits accessible from the backyard.

The bar separated the kitchenette and dining area; it was enormous with a nice long rectangular shape window with a view of the sprawling front yard and passersby! A sliding door was in the wall as you left the Kitchen that closed off the front of the house. It was very James Bond one side matched the kitchen panels the opposite side was white, like the hallway. As soon as you entered the hallway that held the heavy coat closet and Christmas wrapping paper, the flooring was formal. The front door which was to the left, across from the carpeted living room.

I fell in love with the jumbo bay window. The sun shined the brightest in that room. The older I got, the rest of the house was dim. I sat there, often soaking in the sun without a care. Further up, along the long hallway, you opened another door to a carpet that filled a common bathroom that belonged to me and was the guest bathroom when we had visitors, and across from my future siblings' room, the common area carpet flowed to the main bedroom with a full bath.

My room had two windows, one facing the front yard and the other with the view of an apple tree. It was a nice bonus; our yard attracted many kids I met looking out the window.

Momma was now the queen of her throne! She had a ball decorating. The kitchen had pretty white fluffy curtains in the window and the bedroom themes tied into each season. Green velvet couches in the living room were the dressiest space in the house.

Momma invited the family over for dinner, cookouts, and birthday parties.

We continued our same routines. Momma had come into a lifestyle she deserved. A FABULOUS ONE! We were a cute family! I was ready for them to add siblings!

# New Wife, New Life

On weekends my routine was the same as before we moved. I stayed at Nan's; I felt more at home until I eventually adjusted to my new surroundings and made friends.

Momma was creating new traditions because, at Nan's, we never missed church! I had perfect attendance on the church roster. Dressing up for church and dinner on Sunday was tradition. It all took a little getting used to no longer "catching" Coolie at Grandma's in "The Circle on Sundays.

The house was quieter than a mouse peeing on cotton. Gospel Expo with Pastor Nancy Wilson no longer played in the background. Momma and Evan would be asleep. Momma never laid around till 10 and 11 a.m. on the weekends. She was usually up by then, but that also changed.

On Sundays, we missed church; I anticipated the delicious breakfast momma would prepare when she woke up while I watched cartoons. It felt delightful to look at whatever "I" wanted for a change instead of adult tv shows older people liked.

After breakfast, momma allowed me to play during church hours. Like magic in Salem Woods, I had the freedom to roam. I'd never been outside unsupervised. It was fine with me, although the streets were scarce. Down south, families attended church services on Sunday.

Funny, in my old neighborhood, I couldn't leave off the porch, and when I went further than the front yard, momma or Nan had eyes on me till I was out of sight, and Aunt Z took over the watch party from there in her doorway anticipating my arrival.

The same routine occurred when Aunt Z sent Ryan and Chance to our house. They exchanged calls to let each other know we had made it safely.

I guess momma assumed it was a safe neighborhood.

# Adventures of Salem Woods

Marlow was the first friend I met; she was Italian. The first time I had lasagna was with her and her family, and to this day, no one has topped her dad's recipe, not even a restaurant. Dinner took place after the sun went down, and it wasn't even a cookout! I loved it. I liked eating outdoors; momma and I always ate inside unless we had a cookout.

I felt fancy sipping unsweetened tea in the pretty dinner glasses. Nan tea was sweet. I was shocked they omitted the sugar. I didn't want to be rude, so I drank it. The food was so delicious it wasn't bad unsweetened.

Shay lived down the hill across the street from Marlow. He became my best friend! I spent the night at his beautiful home a lot. Pascal, his mom, reminded me of Claire Huxtable. Her haircut was just like mommas! Mrs. P never showed any signs of disdain arriving home to see me on their porch gliding back and forth on the country white swing Sundays after church! If I was the only kid waiting for Shay to come out while they were eating, his mom asked if I'd like to join them.

They were a blended family but symbolized a real family. Shay's older sister came from Detroit, and j treated Jennifer like her birth daughter. Jenifer even called her Mommy. Every other house on Shay row had kids! This end of my block had lots of kids.

The Bope twins moved to the neighborhood, and the kinder twin Kris and I meshed. Unlike "The Circle," the community was full of dogs. I made friends with lots of boys through Shay. I was doing my best not to be scared as we went on adventures through the woods; on days, we jumped the creek behind the golf course cutting through all those backyards. The "flat track" is where we rode on bike trails with hills and dips that made us feel like BMX bike riders! On snow days, the fun continued sliding down the HUGE hills on cardboard and sleds.

# School Daze

My new class had a student named Michelle, so the teacher asked me for a nickname. I decided to go with Mimi, the name they called me, over to Grandma Maury's house.

The teacher sat me at a desk beside a little girl named Teeka. We became friends instantly after she shared crayons with me.

The school was state-of-the-art. The guidance class was across the hall from my class; we went once a week. Oak Summit, the School I transferred from, did not offer guidance classes or mention a guidance counselor. I loved the counselor's beautiful banged haircut; she was very animated and always had a smile.

At the beginning of class, she put on a puppet show with Dusso the Dolphin as we sang along to the song "Hey Dusso, Come on Out!"

The modern library catered to kids, with colorful chairs for kids to lounge and read. Floor-to-ceiling glass windows were the backdrop with a view of the massive playground that offered two baseball fields and dugouts we played kickball on, a basketball court, a hand- painted flat top, monkey bars, and a circular track. My class was in the "new building," South Fork had two buildings. Second grade through fifth grade, located in the school's other wing, was called the "old building," and it smelled old. Upper grades passed by, walking under the catwalk to the "old building."

I eventually started hanging out after school with Teeka; we went to her mom's class right next to our classroom. I always was curious about the teacher's lounge, so I was stoked to accompany Teeka to the lounge to check Mrs. Fox's mailbox and grab a snack in the lounge; I got a Pepsi!

Visits to her house were enjoyable! On days we didn't ride with her mom walking to her house after school was the routine. The walk was fun. I made friends with everyone she introduced me to; the neighborhood had many handsome boys, and I got silent when they were around. They had a different effect on me than my guy friends from my new community.

Teeka made us cinnamon toast to snack on while we watched her favorite soap opera, Santa Barbara. I remember the easy recipe to this day!

Mrs. Fox's large family made God a priority. They ran St. Seater's church, located across from my home church Shiloh Baptist. The entire family moved from Wytheville, Virginia, to North Carolina and resided in the Creekway Community.

The services lasted past 2 p.m.!

On weekends their home was a gathering place for the neighborhood kids, church members, and family! I wish I lived in her neighborhood.

Teeka's Aunt Yandi became my hairstylist. Her salon was in the basement. She did an excellent job! We both could overhear Mrs. Fox's brother's voices rise and fall as they discussed important topics. While my Jheri curl neutralized, she joined them and took a smoke break upstairs. I was too young to make out the discussions, but it seemed important to them.

# New Members Chronicles

Shiloh would always be my home church; momma joined Evan's church. According to history, the church derived from a split downtown at the original location, which occurred once segregation ended. Both churches had the same name First Baptist; the place was 5 minutes away from the entrance of Downtown. The beautiful structure and grounds were similar, on a smaller scale than the now mostly white congregation. It was the boogie, hi-class melanin version that stood out in our community.

Shiloh Baptist Church had all shades of brown faces. Even a child could notice the void of the faces in colors of deep chocolate, it stood out to me tremendously to me in the lightly complected congregate on. I actually had never paid attention to the color of my skin until "momma" joined there.

Service was dull until the preacher spoke unless the Spiritual Choir sang. The congregation came alive as if it were a treat. When they did sing, they stood on the steps leading to the pulpit, which made no sense because the choir that received all the exposure sounded European.

An attendee of hundreds of choir rehearsals, I observed their mouths move and felt nothing.

Still, aside from "Lift Every Voice" Black History Month, their selections were void of the anointing, spirit, and soul—mirroring the atmosphere of the sanctuary. The Spiritual Choir was getting played; they were the better choir, in my opinion, and needed to premier more often; they brought life to the sanctuary every time they sang!

The kid's choir made an appearance every blue moon. An invite to join the Children's Choir wasn't extended personally or via announcements although the church was very charismatic and full of the city's most dignified educators! The lighting of the Advent Candle done by the "same" pretty light skinned children during the holiday season was cool and something I would have loved to participate in but I had no idea how to make that happened. Momma joined the choir and I eventually became an usher. The lady over the usher board was nice. She and her daughter had really pretty Jheri curls.

Thank God the Pastor was on fire when he preached! I liked hearing him speak! He resembled a light-skinned black Jesus with a huge afro, and he roared like Dr. King at the end of his message. Something about his voice made me pick up speed when I could hear him preach from outside on the street as we walked up days we were late.

Sundays, after service, we caught up with Nan at her church. Momma was a wife now and a great cook, so we ate at home on Sunday and were at Nan's for dinner more on holidays. On our first stop, we hung out in her church parking lot till she and Aunt Z got out of service and hollered at them; next, we headed to Evan's godmother's home, walking distance from Nan's church. Evan parent's house was the last stop. I enjoyed the visits. They both offered good snacks. After church, I was always hungry!

# Cousin Zion

Cousin Zion was one year older than me, raised as an only child, and bossy! The ponytails she donned were pretty and lengthy on her relaxed tresses! We became family once momma and Evan married! I think we cured each other's "only child" syndrome and she loved her Nannie like I loved Nan! Their dynamic duo was like the bonds between me, momma, and Nan before Evan proposed. Shonda Mae, Zion's mom was the only girl of all her brothers and lived diagonally across the street from her mother.

Nannie's house was so large she leased rooms to boarders! Willy Mabe's is the restaurant she named after herself, the most delicious collard greens were sold at her place!

I visited Zion often on weekends.

Saturday nights went to the skating rink; while we dressed for the rink, I could tell if Shonda Mae had "company" arriving after she dropped us off at the rink. The clothes horse had outfits to select from hanging around her room.

Momma and I hadn't ever lived in a place with just the two of us. They were chillin! Shonda Mae's house was sickening, she did her own interior decorating and furniture upholstering.

The boutique owner quit what most call "that good job" at the telephone company she worked for years to go into business for herself.

Sunday, Zion and I woke up and lounged around, talking and laughing about the fun we had the night before while the scent of the big brunch Shonda Mae was preparing filled the air. They weren't big churchgoers but loved God.

I lingered in the kitchen, stuck in the chair full as she prepared dinner. I learned how to make her delicious collards; one of the main ingredients was the bacon grease from brunch! She added a pinch of sugar, seasoned the liquid, and added the clean-cut greens that melted down nicely and tender in the pot.

The environment was very relaxed; everyone let their hair down here. Shonda Mae was good peeps!

# The Gem

South Fork gym after-school program is where I went until momma got off work. Talent was cultivated here by many kids. I cheered for The Wolfpack in their basketball league! Weekly Arts and Crafts classes, ice cream parties, and access to the open gym kept me busy those two hours I was there until Momma got off of work. I met many kids, and Teeka's older brother and cute friends would come to the gym to brush up on basketball, breakdance on the stage, and spin fast on the cardboard in their wind suits. I learned how to play ball and breakdance from observing.

I enjoyed meeting new friends I didn't have access to during the school day at the gym after school! There was a soda machine in the gym too!

# Shift in the Atmosphere

Evan worked the second shift; the volume on TV coming from the den signaled his arrival home.

As my momma and I slept, he entered my room "checking" on me, I thought. I didn't grow up with a man in the house or a dad, so I assumed this is what went on when you had a family, similar to "The Beavers" on television show. The parents checked in on the boys, but they did not touch or tuck them as they slumbered. Nan and momma never interrupted my rest either.

Hoping it was a bad dream, covers would come back down towards my collarbone, causing me to awake from the breeze of air as the sheets suctioned my body.

I was really afraid when I felt a draft on my body from the navel up as if my pajama top was lifting.

In denial, I'd lay frozen, and I unfroze as my eyes examined how differently the organization of the covers was from my usual slumber pattern, confirming it wasn't a dream. He got so sloppy I saw him quietly tiptoeing hurriedly out of my room as if I didn't know he was there, closing the door slowly but gently until it clicked shut behind him. This so-called "tuck-in" continued, and I began to awaken often with him over me, instantly going into a paralyzed state from visibly seeing him fixing my covers, still unsure of what he was doing was called! I knew something was wrong once I felt someone touching my chest.

The creepiness had to stop. I came up with a great idea. My bedroom door thankfully opened to a 2-sided square that formed a box at a 50- degree angle when the door was open. I placed the right side of my desk chair flush against the wall in the box area. I tilted the chair forward and pressed the back edge against the door situating the front chair legs against the baseboard of the floor. The other two chair legs rested against the wall behind it. Feeling secure with the chair locked and "no give" if someone tried to enter a child isn't aware of Fire Hazards.

I started sleeping with my desk chair behind my door.

Evan and I weren't even on that level so this "I'm married and a new stepdaddy checking in on my stepdaughter before I turn in skit" gave me discomfort.

Momma never asked why the chair was behind the door the first morning she struggled to get in and wake me up for school. Did she not wonder who I was trying to keep out or find this behavior strange?

# The Choice of a New Generation

2nd-grade boys with fresh haircuts and lotion face captured my eye. Some were well-groomed all the time; others just looked nice on the first day of school and picture day. As a future hairstylist, I appreciated mothers who ensured their children were well groomed.

My love for Pepsi was out of control. Nan had me walk to Mr. Mack's to get her a Pepsi and Salem Cigarettes. The bottle called my name whenever I was in the kitchen alone; I'd open the refrigerator, and it would say, drink me, so without permission, I'd steal a few sips.

It was a hot day at the end of my 3rd grade school year. Mrs. Colon's bottle of Tab soda was out on her desk with tiny sweat beads, I could tell it was cold, and I took a swig of it in front of the entire class on the day she left momentarily. No one told!!!

# Detour to the Kitchen

Evan ass started waking up with us in the morning. It felt like punishment for barricading my room door. Most 2nd shift workers that stayed up late slept in the morning. He didn't have to work until 4 o'clock!

Perched at the bar one morning as I exited the bathroom sat Evan! Shocked, I immediately backed in and shut the door, then hit the light switch. In pitch black, digesting the fact this boogie man was at the opposite end of the hallway, unable to touch me but now attempting to view me from the kitchen, made my heart race! Momma kept the door to the bedroom area closed in the morning for heating purposes, so it had no business open! I tried staying in the bathroom, listening for the scrape of the barstool legs as a sign he got up from the bar. Momma left before my bus came. I had to get dressed before she left! My new routine would consist of peeking out to see if the coast was clear because I didn't have a housecoat; momma had hers on every morning and since, though, so with just a towel to wrap around me, I'd dash to the bathroom and after I was done crack the door with the light off then dash straight to my room. My heart would beat as I danced with anxiety every morning, so I started closing the door where the carpet stopped that led to the hallway to the kitchen and took my clothes to the bathroom with me. Other than "that," life "seemed" normal.

# A Blessing Arrives

Momma was finally pregnant, but her blood pressure was up, and doctors hospitalized her with toxemia. I was sleeping when Evan woke me up to tell me Momma was in labor. Half asleep, I made my way to the car. He was driving beyond the speed limit to drop me off at Nan's and make it to the hospital for the birth. When we arrived, she was on the porch with her coat and purse, ready to go to the hospital.

Emily was born a month early. She favored mom with lots of hair; I'd brush every chance I could get making sure to be careful with her soft spot. Momma would repeatedly say, "Hold her head."

Emily was precious. I was so glad to be her big sister! Evan was beaming with pride. He took pictures of Emily with hundred-dollar bills around her when she was a few days old. It was my first time seeing one-hundred-dollar bills, let alone multiples! I didn't express it to him; I wanted to touch the money, but he wasn't friendly. He was enjoying his firstborn; I knew I wasn't his child, but he acted like that wasn't my little sister we could both enjoy together as I waited for him to finish. The room was quiet. I watched the entire photoshoot. He moved about as if I wasn't there as I waited for what felt like my "turn" to play with Emily. Dude didn't take not one shot of me or the two of us together like a mature adult in the presence of sisters. The time he and momma had me take a picture of them with Emily holding hands was the craziest though! The camera had a timer they could've captured the moment a weekend I stayed at Nan's; the timing was terrible! I'm guessing this bonus photo was personal. It clarified "he had one child."

Evan often let me know without speaking that I wasn't his child despite the vows he made with God and momma.

# Childish

Miss Creekway showed up mid-school year to my 4th-grade class. Cussing was a no-no at my house, so when I overheard her cuss and told the teacher we became enemies, it wasn't long before we became excellent friends!

The first time we went to pick Miss Creekway up for an outing, my new best friend came out of the house rocking mismatch earrings, one BIG hoop, and a diamond earring like Janet Jackson. Demetria, her big sister, was always fashionably correct; I'd mirror my big sis if I had one! The sidewalk was like a runway. As she made her way to the car, Momma began to make that sound in a siren pitch I'd heard from women in our family when a woman exuded sexiness, was inappropriately dressed, even possibly dressed in something women raised in Christian households don't have the nerve to wear. She gave closer to the car. Compared to my string bean-looking body, momma was caught off guard by this 4th grader. I guess?

The women were wrong for judging others that had no control over their shapes. Why were they like this towards certain females? She was six months younger than me, just mature for her age.


Miss Creekway started coming to my house and saved me from getting in trouble once. The genius gave me the idea to drop a pink slip from our teacher in the tub and then give it to my momma after it dried. Momma was always rushing in the morning, so I had her sign without knowing what it stated; she didn't have time to question me or make out what the water-stained area said. It worked!

# The First 48 In "The Skin I'm in"

South Fork Elementary had been a pleasant experience until Kris crashed his bike with me on the back while speeding by the dog Spanky's house, known for chasing kids. Kris was scratched up and poorly skinned; I had a few scratches, but he had apparent scratches; you could see blood on his white skin after we landed on an unpaved driveway with about 2 feet of rocks. Afterward, we both walked home as friends, or so I thought. Monday at school, the principal voice came over the classroom speaker requesting me to the office. They closed the office door, and the blonde female principal with masculine features like the Russian lady in Rocky and the assistant principal the entire school said had no ass questioned me about the accident as if I had caused it. They explained Kris had gone to the hospital. I'm thinking, okay and????? The incident happened on a Sunday away from the school! I was confused and mad. "THE SCHOOL PRINCIPAL" had embarrassed me by calling my name over the speaker in front of the class, and I was very uncomfortable hemmed up in that office as they questioned me. That Monday was my first brush with discrimination, I realized later.

# Bait

"I have something to show you," Evan said to me one afternoon as I encountered him in that dreaded common area on the carpet that led to the hallway of the kitchen. I stood there, froze, staring at him speechlessly, thinking, "No, you don't!" The thought had volumes of a shout that had a silencer on it. I lost hearing like eardrums can do when shots fire! Whatever "something" was, I was NOT finding out. I went to my room immediately till he left for work, listening for "he leaving" sounds; his car finally backed out of the driveway. What kind of daddy even step doesn't say goodbye to a 12-year-old they are leaving home alone? According to his actions, one with a plan that doesn't coincide with parenting.

I immediately called momma at work and told her what he said and about him watching me when I was leaving the bathroom. SHE DIDN'T SAY MUCH at all. After I hung up, my eyes went to the ironing board; unsatisfied with momma's response, I walked straight to it and plugged up the iron. When it got hot, I tattooed the kitchen wall. When asked how it got there, I told my first lie and said my sister did it. I was a good girl; burning the wall was a horrible thing, but so was baiting a child, now that I think about it. My mom wasn't verbal about the situation. She took action!!!!!! The kitchen sliding door was closed shut when I entered and got out of the shower the following day and after that. I felt safer. I also stayed after school as much as possible; when I got off the activity bus, my momma would be home, and

Evan would be gone to work. I loved her so much. I felt good when he was gone!

Summer friends weren't allowed over unless my momma was home; I didn't know why but I got an idea when I looked back and saw Evan on the porch staring at my older teenage friend Kathy and me as we walked down the street. Evan had me confused. Her younger sister and I played all the time and watched us down the road, definitely not when my mom was around, but who knows? She was still with him after she knew he had been inappropriate with me. He was no father figure to me anyway, looking at my friends!

# Grammy Award

On days school was out, my cousins and I went to our babysitter's house.

Aunt Z discovered Ms. Betsy. Her sons loved her! I fell in love with her too when she started babysitting me! She wasn't just a sitter; she became my third grandma in the neighborhood. My cousins being there made it a bonus! Ms. Betsy wouldn't be up, so our knock at the door was her alarm. Once inside, as if the snooze button minutes were ticking away, the sitter shifted back down the hallway in her slides to her bedroom. We sat there respectfully and quietly. I wondered why she didn't turn on the television for us. The slippers on her feet sounded like sandpaper shifting on the wooden floor as she reentered, passing by us to sit on the couch in circular dip serving as a thrown. No one sat there but her! Prayer and meditation took place on the sofa every morning, followed by a lower lip fill with fresh snuff. Next, Ms. Betsy turned on what her era called the component set to start the day with gospel music.

I sang along to the familiar songs while the boys played with toys they brought from home; the obituaries came on following the gospel show with theme music spewing the most beautiful harmony I'd ever heard from a song called "Be Not Dismayed"! At noon the news came on. The babysitter's teenage niece Solange was awake by then; she was the big sister I always wanted! I'd sing along with her to the R&B music on her radio, watching her put on makeup. Solange entered me into talent shows at the recreation center. The first time I sang "I Found Love on a Two-Way Street." I got a standing ovation.

The teen boys and men stopped what they were doing when she passed as we entered the recreation center and stores. She and all her friends had style! I enjoyed listening in on their conversations like little sisters do. I hung out with her after nap time while Ms. Betsy watched Days of Oour Lives and whatever followed every day and in that order. Momma picked me up a little after 5pm.

Ms. Betsy is the first hustler I met. She was self-made. Cash was plentiful! Ice cream cone sales at her back door accumulated tremendous amounts of change that covered half the kitchen table, and the dollar bills were tucked safely in her bra. The ice cream house was jumping. Kids started knocking on the back door after 10 for a "cone of cream," she called it! The bank wasn't privy to the ice cream sales or babysitting revenue; Ms. Betsy stored the money under the mattress and couch cushions.

I loved when we went on grocery store trips. Ms. Betsy set Raid Roach Bombs before Mr. Joe, the neighborhood driver with a bright idea before driving apps, pulled up in his station wagon to take us to Food World. The house was smoggy, and dead roaches were everywhere, like a war zone when we returned. My cousins and I helped bring in all the flavors of ice cream and food she purchased.

A Full course dinner simmered after she stocked up on groceries.

We snapped the peas on the front porch for the meal. I learned how to make egg custard from my sitter/third grandma.

Speaking of grandma, I could see Nan creep on the porch watering her plants three doors to the left from Ms. Betsy's porch days; she was off from work and wondered why she wasn't watching us!

We never misbehaved and knew not to play with her because she cussed when she was mad. LOL. She had girlfriends who would stop by, and if a lie came up during their conversation, she would say SHIIIIIIIIIIIIIIIIT drawing the word out extra-long!! A good neighbor friend Ms. Roxie was so beautiful but reeked of urine. You could smell the scent of pee like an oil burner plugin walking up to and past her sidewalk leading to her door. It was the first time I encountered a woman that hadn't bathed. She was lovely, so I ignored the smell. My cousins and I would discuss and laugh about it sometimes.

Ms. Betsy's nieces and a nephew my age who were there; Desiree, Sonya, and Bryson, were also my age, and we all became great friends. Bryson was so cute he had a beautiful abstract birthmark that made his face stand out in the crowd. I got butterflies being so close to him at nap time; Ms. Betsy was so into her stories she didn't pay us any mind we were "innocent kids."

# Hello Brooklyn

I was the BIG sister of two girls now. Brooklyn was born in December with a head rooted with dense coils I loved to play in. Finding my way through the thick maze of hair to her scalp was a task and assisted in exposing me to a texture! Brooklyn was so strong before she even arrived here! The way she moved in momma's belly was shocking. Momma didn't know the sex of the baby. Brooklyn was so active in the womb they proclaimed a boy was on the way. Evan was in expectancy of a boy he repeatedly called a football player. Brooklyn was a beautiful sweet baby full of energy whose smile lit up the room! She was the perfect light skin blend of momma and Evan. Everyone thought she and Emily were twins. I had plans for my sisters; they were like live baby dolls I could play with whenever I wanted. Being the only child was boring once momma married; I begged for brothers and sisters, and four years later, I had 2!

# Rude Awakening

Rise and shine to specific instructions from Evan "not to use my bathroom the water was "being repaired" confused me... My God, it was too early for this, I had just woken up. Evan had never been that eager to share news with me; I CRINGED at the BAD NEWS! Fear gripped at the thought of me showering in their bathroom while momma was at work. I was positive she was unaware of this so-called work on the "water"?

All the problem and resolution skills I accumulated from Evan's sporadic obstacle courses were making me nuts; now a water issue had arisen.

How was I going to dodge this new dart he threw?

The clock was ticking while my friends played outside and I watched morning fade.

The desire to eat and watch television or play no longer mattered. Feeling trapped inside, I just wanted to bathe; at this point!

Wondering how I was going to get into that bathroom consumed me.

Quietly for what seemed like hours, I listened to his movements as usual. Once the lawn mower cranked I dashed through their bedroom into the bathroom for the dreadful shower FULLY DRESSED!!!

Adjusting the shower head, I tilted it in the highest arch possible so the water would sprout out far as the water drowned out the sound of the lawnmower.

The decision to close the blinds made it impossible to view Evan without the blinds shifting.

In "Stretch Armstrong" mode, I extended my long neck like an ostrich in the direction of the window, my lower torso closest to the sprouting water, as I soaped up.

The unorthodox shower consisted of an eye exercise taking quick peeks to the left and darting at the doorknob to the right. Without touching the blinds my eyes zoned in on him through the circular holes that held the blinds together.

Mad momma left me in the care of Evan ALONE suddenly the doorknob I SPECIFICALLY LOCKED started to move, and the hair stood up on my body! Thank God the towel was close. Heart beating like crazy, I hurried and wrapped up in the corner behind the door as he jiggled till the lock popped open! Triangle in behind the opened door I stood there covered, to his surprise, towel clenched tight and unyankable, steaming MAD at the realization he was trying to catch me undressed like the women he looked at in the nasty magazines!!!!!!!!! I glared at him like the crazy scorpion he was! "O" is all he could muster up to say then exited closing the door behind him.

I exhaled releasing the anxiety, from another "FAILED" LUST-filled booby trap he set for me.

What the hell did he mean? "O??" The fool violated me unlocking that door!

I saw red I wanted blood!!!!!!

This man was trying to catch me naked but the disgusting plan FAILED, NO WEAPON EVAN FORMED AGAINST ME SHALL PROSPER; IT WON'T WORK!!!!

After listening intently for noise or the slightest movement in momma's room the den door shut, finally out of hell I looked out the window and the car backed out the driveway; I WAS FREE!!!!!

My stomach was in knots as I held the phone receiver in my hand dialing momma's work extension. I regretted the call, like all the others no emotion; she didn't say anything in defense of me like, "it's on when I see him!"

Sweat beads appeared on my toes as my body boiled at the reminder I hadn't heard from my momma all day!

The water company was a no-show and our faucets and water was working fine like the day prior.

My eyes fixated on his precious fish and as if in a Trans since I couldn't put my hands on Evan, I began trashing the den, first giving the fish tank a side karate chop and cracking the glass, scaring his fish as he scared me all dam day! Next, I grabbed the exotic fish from the fish tank and gave it the hot bath Evan deprived me excited he would find them floating dead after work tonight.

I prided myself on keeping the commandments I learned in church but there were consequences for his behavior. What a shame I had committed an act of violence based on that monster's actions.

The Bible says confusion comes from the enemy; Evan was "THE ENEMY"!!

# The Bird Flew from the Coo-coos Nest

Coolie sister Ann lived on our street; the only road I had to cross to get to her was the one beside my house, and her house was 28 houses down.

Aunt Ann was big on saving souls and intentional about church membership. Once a drive all the way to Charlotte North Carolina from Winston-Salem fulfilled  experience she desired. Like a niece, I ran to my auntie, thinking she could save me from Evan; unfortunately, I was wrong. I did, however, get my first ride ever in her car when she returned me home like a good Christian shouldn't.

I wasn't in trouble for leaving undetected when she returned me, and to me, it was a low-key sign of guilt.

My thoughts were all over the place as I sat in my room

Looking at the brighter side of things, I learned blood wasn't thicker than water.  Stranger's to family they call "new converts" had preeminence above family members.

Recognition and praise from pastors for bringing soul's to God fuel  leaders to create blueprints to fix  strangers in need while  their own blood relation needs go ignored even a child.

Who knows maybe I avoided the foster care system that day.  Wondering if she had told Coolie about the visit; he was 7-10 minutes away and could've rescued me in my dreams, but in reality, neither came to see me before I ran away so be it.

I had to remember I was the invisible family member.

# Girls & Boys Club

## DAY PARTY

Evans's coworker's kids went to the Girl's and Boys' clubs. Once Zion started going, I joined the summer program. It was $25, covering each girl until the following summer, including after-school care! Momma and Evan took advantage of this perk during the school year on days school was closed. Summer was the best season girls came from all over! Kids from the Southside of the city and those in the school district of the club went year-round. I'd take hair supplies from home and braid hair. I loved it!

Zion arrived before me; there wasn't a morning I'd arrived a Pepsi was not in her possession! I made lots of friends, but I bonded with a group of friends at the Foosball Table! My favorite game partner was Zane. She was competitive and athletic! We enjoyed playing against Sasha and Tasha, Mia and Sonya, and occasionally cousins Zion and Kia when Zion and I were not teamed up. Zion and I got along well; she was a blessing. It was so hard to believe we were cousins through marriage and not blood!

# It Is What It Is

That Christmas, I awoke to what looked like someone got a raise because a lot of what I asked Santa for was in the den. Cabbage Patch doll whose two ponytails I rearranged in a cute shirt, jeans, and a fitted orange windbreaker with sneakers. Teddy Ruxpin, pretty much everything a kid my age dreamed of, was there. I filled out the adoption papers for my new daughter. Before 7 am, momma brought to my attention the Cabbage Patch doll I kissed so hard after unwrapping; my lip swollen and Teddy Ruxpan were my sisters. She and Evan were putting them up for when the girls got older. I had fun playing with the items while it lasted. My gifts consisted of clothing and stuff but not the hottest items of the season right there for me to touch! None of my gifts had the value of the two toys they removed from the room and returned to bed. I caught an attitude. My sisters weren't old enough to enjoy the Cabbage Patch Doll. I realized I was a "stepchild" on that day! My dad didn't ask me what I wanted.

I would run into him at Grandma Maury's later, but I knew not to expect anything.

Exchanging gifts after dinner at Nan's became my highlight! Evan's family gave me presents too. Not doing so would've been embarrassing to them.

# Jada Kisses

Jada Evan's sister was my favorite aunt on his side. We hung out, ate, and went shopping, & my first pair of designer jeans and 1st concert experience in Charlotte are all thanks to Jada! I love how she treated me like a real niece, practically daughter, and she never pretended Jada was unabashedly herself! She liked to have a good time and would arrive at our house after drinking hours, sometimes with a male friend, and that same smell that oozed under Uncle Miles's door came from the living room. I liked the scent! I woke up and tiptoed to the den. The coffee table looked like "Weekend at Bernie's! " Drinks with ice were still on the coffee table. I took a sip of the glass half full that looked like fresh Pepsi and realized it was Hennessy and Coke and spit it out. It was worse than the Club Soda on top of the fridge I tasted because it had the word soda on the bottle.

Any man she introduced us to would be so fine. Travels in the army allowed her to purchase furniture from other countries imported to the US. Church with Jada was an event. I would be so nervous about our arrival time because although she was an adult, as a child hairdresser, you were brave or glamourous relaxing your edges or washing hair 2 hours or less before service started. Cream square- shaped nails accompanied her perfectly curled shortcut! Perfume and outfit would make you look. We would get to church 45 minutes late. She was a visitor; they probably thought she drove from Charlotte that morning, not that she was already in town and had gone out the night before. So it was excellent; everyone was just happy to see her! Auntie was dressed like Alexis Carrington from Dynasty, chatting real proper in the sanctuary as if she got to church on time. On cue, shades appeared as the conversation lingered outside; the designer shades slid on smoothly before hugs to long-time friends she didn't see inside! I'm guessing my momma and Evan slept in while I was hanging with "Jada" the fun never ended! She and Evan were indeed related.

She loved visiting after church! We went to their favorite cousin's house, Shonda Mae!

I played with Zion while she and Shonda Mae cut up, like when I visited on weekends.

They talk men and fashion about Shonda Mae many projects she was working on.

All of women in Evan's family owned sewing machines and were talented in décor and clothing design.

Aunt Shail selected me to be a flower girl for her wedding that she made all of the dresses for each person in the wedding party. She created home décor for momma.

I was getting my fair share of pizza from Evan's sisters! Jada ordered a large supreme pizzas from Pizza Hut for lunch at Shonda Mae's boutique.

Countess Evans's youngest sister knows I loved pizza and brought me pizza on Friday nights after she and her Winston Salem State's a basketball teammates popped up close to 11 right before Evan got off work.

It was so cool to have the players over at the house.

# Progressive Vibes

Evan washed the car Sunday mornings and goofed around playing loud jazz as if we didn't have church soon. Nan didn't even allow you to wash clothes on Sunday. Evan followed "his" rules seven days a week, although Saturday would've been a better day when we pulled up; the car matched the other shiny cars on the church lot.

During story hour, all the kids left the sanctuary; oddly, Momma and Evan made me stay with them while adults listened to the Reverend preach. Maybe they were scared I'd mention some of Evans's statements made to me or the water repair day?

The Forester's Evan parents had a house built in the Carver High School district. They had that Benz in the new pastel yellow with a beige leather interior I enjoyed riding in. The homes were sprawling and beautiful, I admit, void of the noisy life in The Circle, aka "the projects" I preferred. Everyone was proper. Kids were scarce. Retirees filled the area. The one young person in the neighborhood was The Forester's neighbor's daughter Robyn. She was older and constantly reading books; her single mom, a psychiatrist, was grooming her for success. Everyone, including the Foresters, was rooting for her.

Evan was doing a great job mocking his parents. We were mini versions of them.

HONEY, his momma, could cook like her sister Willy Mabe! I spent the night and awakened to the most delicious breakfast there!!!! Don't get me wrong, my grandmothers could cook their butt off, but all the meals here were fancy! Food was transferred to a serving dish and displayed nicely on the table. Lunch was like dinner, and dinners were like Sunday meals, even if it wasn't Sunday! Mrs. Forester had a lovely garden out back, and fresh vegetables sat in the kitchen sink window during the warm months.

I like the lifestyle they lead! My hair skills improve by playing with dolls at home and doing my classmates' hair every year of elementary school; if the opportunity arose. I knew I had to be a hairstylist in the heart when I used the combs the photographer supplied and combed everybody's hair on the fifth-grade picture day.

I mimicked the stylist at the salon after watching them apply relaxers, roll, and style hair. Nan always liked her scalp oiled with Fashion Fare light hair oil before rolling her hair with sponge rollers lined with toilet paper to protect the hair.

My decision to become a hairstylist would allow me to live the same way or better when I grew up.

# Growing Pains

My stomach ached. Momma was at work; she told me to lie down. My friends and I picked blackberries earlier, and I had eaten too many. When I went to tinkle, I saw red. I called momma back to tell her what happened, and she told me my menstrual cycle had come. I didn't know what a menstrual cycle was or the purpose of its arrival. When she arrived home, she gave me a white belt and what she called a "sanitary napkin" with floppy loose ends long enough to turn the actual sanitary napkin into a halter top and tie the floppy ends behind my back. Momma adjusted the belt around my waist and looped the loose ends into the belt, holding the pad in place. I hated it!

# I See Me

Middle school my day started early! The bus ride to school to the city's Eastside took 25 minutes. The bus speedometer was set at 35 all the cars went around us on the highway we went so slow.

The age or grade of some students was hard to say because they looked so mature. Wow, I felt like a string bean. I was no longer throwing on anything; my appearance began to matter more and I was checking myself out in the mirror after I out together an outfit like momma.

There wasn't much I could do about my 3-inch Jheri curl. My hair was growing out nicely before momma called herself to save money and touched up my Jheri Curl with leftover product from Evan's texturizer curly kit! My hairstyle was not the look of a future hairstylist. Debuting the look at the Girls Club was a disaster. The short hair got me picked on by a few girls. Better there than here!

Zane from the Girl's Club was in my class; that was a plus!! I made friends with a brilliant girl named Stacy with hands that belonged in a Dawn or Palmolive commercial. Her well-kept fingernails were always polished nicely and caught my eyes as she turned her book pages. The straight-A student prioritized her studies.

Middle School was different; the kids liked to fight. Some even frightened me and seemed so angry. Some cute guys were in the class, too, looking at you up, down, and around, so when I was on my cycle, I ensured the thick maxi pad didn't make me look square from behind.

Neighborhood friends got off the bus at my stop and gathered at the house to watch music videos and dance after. The VCR always stayed paused in case a video I wanted to record came on. Making sure I wasn't recording over something important that belonged to momma or Evan during a fast forward I came across a nude lady that poured milk over her chest in a bathtub full of milk. I ejected the tape immediately, knowing it had to belong to Evan.

I caught Jami and Kristi, my friend from down the road kissing by the carpeted common area near my bathroom. I knew she didn't have to use it when I saw them head that way! I didn't realize Jami liked white girls. "I" hadn't even kissed in my house yet, and they were tongue kissing like the preacher said you may now kiss the bride. I heard you had to kiss very safely with a person that wore braces.

Jami had braces and they kissed like pros.

Wonder if it was the spirit of lust that loomed in our house from or if they were intrigued by the explicit video we accidentally came across.

Everybody's footprints would be removed with the vacuum before momma came home.

# Discovery Zone

I got into recording music videos heavily on Evan's VCR tapes and discovered porn.

My momma's closet was full of lovely things I modeled when home alone. I'd dance like she would when she tried new clothes after popping the tags. The handbags were full of ice cream truck change!

Momma stored the pregnancy book she referenced when expecting in her closet. After reading specific chapters, I didn't want to have children. The book brake down of the baby's route on delivery day was painful to view. Nude pictures of couples positioned as if they were in a Twister game were towards the end of the book. The paragraph explained these positions helped with labor. Whatever those couples were doing, I also decided to pass on.

I'd raid Evan's closet, too, mostly when momma's change was low. The empty Halston Lotion bottle was the piggy bank that sat on his chest of drawers until he called himself hiding in the closet; once he tired of me taking all the silver coins out.

Evan's closet had a stack of magazines on the shelf. Over time I read several of the magazine articles from the GQ and Playboy magazine on very various subjects. The unfamiliar sexual subjects made my heart race fast as I turned the pages. One piece gave instructions on how to turn on the bath water, get up under the faucet and let the water run down over your opened legs. I tried it at bath time and afterwards decided to keep the instructions from the article a secret.

# Brown Girl Joy

I knew Salem Woods like the back of my hand, and it had become very diverse! So many black families moved in, and I always made new friends! My friend Strawberry and I were walking; on our stroll, she spoke to a young lady with long relaxed hair that swayed as she stood and walked toward us while Strawberry explained to me their brothers played soccer together. After introducing me to a young lady named Trista, she joined us on our walk. The three of us walked half the block, and another melanated young lady was in her driveway like kindred spirits; after saying hi and introducing Ari and me, they shared their moms were friends.

We discussed our schools; they were lucky to attend schools outside the district. It was fun to ask about people I knew from their schools, realizing we had lots of friends in common. We chatted for so long that it started to get dark.

Strawberry attended church frequently and was close to her grandmother like I was with Nan! When she wasn't at home or church, she most likely was visiting her grandmother. Our walk was a rare occasion. I had fun and looked forward to revisiting them someday!

# God Help Me

Life was not like a box of chocolates. On outings, I preferred sitting behind the passenger seat momma had no idea how uncomfortable I was sitting between my sisters' car seats in the Peugeot. Evan adjusted the mirror way down and veered in it even when he wasn't backing up like The Goonies movie character changed his rearview mirror to look at the girl's chest or down her shirt in the backseat. Evan made me ashamed of the developing process of my body. My solution to get out of the creep's view was crossing my arms over my blossoming chest area and sliding to the right as far as I could, car seat there and all!!

Momma was oblivious to my discomfort but very delighted about Evan's shift reassignment since he was home at night with "her."

Reading and comprehending complex math word problems was difficult for me. Momma grouped me with this man knowing all the complaints I had against him! She could recognize how beneficial his math skills were and block out encounters and behaviors he exhibited in my presence while she was asleep or not at home.

He was crafty with math and computers; he tried to assist me, but his patience was short. I'll never forget the smell of his breath as it passed my nostrils. I was getting impatient, it was hard to stomach him. Of all the dam people to teach me; I couldn't understand why we hadn't abandoned him and that HOUSE OF LUST!!!

7th-grade health class opened my eyes to human psychology, anatomy, sexuality, and sex education. Boys started to like me, look at me and call me on the phone. Without the assistance of family, I began to question Evan's motives and gestures at Prepubescent me. Every day I had to wonder what or if he had some weird info or made-up lie to have me discombobulated.

Daycare wasn't cheap. I got a glimpse of paper with a long list of figures that calculated the bills. Without asking or paying me they decided to cut corners and turn me into the free babysitter!

Evan was back on the second shift this particular summer. He ordered me to make lunch for my sisters. My energy was, I'm not your slave. While he slept, I made the sandwiches with disdain for him. He came to inspect the food, then yelled at me because my sisters' sandwiches didn't have mayo and accused me of making them dry sandwiches. These were my sisters, not my kids'; hell, I was a kid who by the way DID NOT eat cold-cut sandwiches! Outside of tuna in the summer, we ate three hot meals a day at Nan's house!!!   Adults prepared the meals; I knew Evan was not an adult!!!! I would eat when my momma got home. This man wasn't a good candidate for step-parenting!!!!!

Momma had no business leaving me in his care! The pattern of delusion she created forced me to lose respect for her slowly but surely. Times like this caused me to wonder how she could stay with a man terrorizing her child; it burdened me.

# Upperclassman

On the first day of eighth grade, I thought I had made it to the top!

First-year students only came to the eighth-grade hall on the third floor of the three-story building to go to the library. I arrived at school in a long acid-washed jean skirt, a white ten-button shirt with army green pen stripes, and fresh white pointed-toe Kapers, no socks.

No one told me I was smart. The barometer was being in classes lots of European students sprinkled with a handful of melanin. I shopped where they shopped and pretty much was comfortable and satisfied in the life momma had dreamed for us. It was a beautiful life I could've considered perfect if Evan wasn't so full of perversion! Nice car, middle-class neighborhood, beautiful family, hair salon visits every two weeks, and a dog named Charlie.

I no longer had that greasy Jheri curl; I had a relaxer, and momma gave me control over my hairstyle options. Alexander was our hairstylist.

Going to the school exposed me to a town near Winston called Clemmons. I had a few friends that lived there and a sister girl I meshed with named Talena that was fly as all get out from "my side of town!"

Her mom was the coolest, not because she was in school to be a hairstylist but because she got us matching outfits for the annual Carver High school Spring Talent Show. I'll never forget it! This girl reenacted the Pleasure Principle video so well that not even the Fly Girls that danced on In Living Color could out-dance her performance!

Talena had a sharp, symmetrical haircut, short stacked on one side, and the other hung over her eye so long she had a signature swing she did to get it out of her face as it fell to her shoulder. Our hairstylist was friends and her mom did hair and we just clicked PERIOD!

Fashion was the goal met daily by the trendsetter! I loved that we both loved to dance and she was a dancing machine!

I asked for a Honda Spree Scooter and waterbed like hers that Christmas. Christmas break I spent time at her house until Christmas Eve. Evan's daddy's truck was outside when I got home! I just knew my Honda Spree was inside. To my surprise, a "Super Single" heated waterbed encased in light brown glossy Cherrywood awaited me. I loved the bed and looked forward to selecting pretty curtains and bedding from momma's J C Penney catalog. I felt older. I could tell High school was right around the corner.

# Unattended Children

At the end of eighth grade, mom and Evan became homeowners; we moved to a neighborhood about 3 miles away. My dad's residence was closer now, 4 minutes away by car; if we had a more intimate relationship, I would've ridden my bike; the distance was short! I liked the house a lot; my bathroom was in my room instead of beside it!!!! The school district was full of friends I grew up with from "The Circle!" I also had a boyfriend, Connor that lived in the school district; we met at the mall. Connor's beautiful dark skin and features were similar to Coolie and my granddaddies on my momma's side. Nan always said it's in the DNA seemingly, I like momma, and Nan had a thing for chocolate!

Living on opposite sides of town; the only times I could see him was Mondays when he pulled up on his Honda Spree at my church to kick it during momma's choir rehearsal, and we linked up at the mall on weekends.

Connor was ready to take it to the next level; being around him made me giddy! Summer before ninth grade, my virginity was broken by Connor; the pain made sex nothing to look forward to doing again after the first experience. I was babysitting my sisters and snuck him in. They were banging on the door as if they knew I was in pain as my knee hit the door a lot during the occurrence. I felt strange afterward and noted that sex was more pleasurable for males, not females!

It was not my first time at the rodeo; the only difference is this attempt was successful. Embarrassingly seventh grade, I fell for a cute gray- eyed curly-haired, light skin boy name Juan that resided across the street from my classmate Stacy. We talked on the phone a lot, and one day I went to his house after school, and we attempted to do the nasty, but GOD BLOCKED IT!!! His buddy spread a rumor around the entire school that I was tight after Juan told him what we "tried."

# Flag Girls

Miss Creekway was on the flag team and made me aware they needed girls, so I joined and committed to a week of 40-hour band camp. I enjoyed it; her dad stayed minutes from campus and picked us up for lunch. Momma only purchased breakfast from Hardee's; since this was the closest fast-food restaurant, this is where he took us for lunch. He ordered us Chicken Sandwich Combos. It was delicious! Her dad was doing well; he owned a club and was very handsome. He favored my childhood doctor, Dr. Kennedy. Mrs. Hubbard made our flag uniforms. I was an official flag girl. It was a blessing because I met a lot of upperclassmen on the flag team, many of who dated football players on the varsity team. Connor was a water boy! He was well-known and could get away with it. I, on the other hand, was turned off being the

I held my excitement in—especially when we rode the activity bus together after practice and after Friday night games. Some of the guys flirted with me on the low. I liked one of them.

# Amid The Pines

RJR, Society Hill, was a well-equipped school known for wealth nestled "amid the pines. The bus route to school had lots of beauty to take in. The closer we got to the school, the larger the square footage of the vast homes was. It was shaping my values.

In the first year of high school at RJR, I accumulated an after-school clientele of students that admired my hairstyles. I began to provide hair care after school in my bedroom.

Miss Creekway and I had homeroom and Driver's Education together, where we met a new friend named Janet! Connor knew Janet; they had been going to school together for years! We all clicked, and the two of them hung out together more often because I, of course, clung to my boyfriend. Inseparable, we walked to all my classes together. I discovered he was a popular guy.

# After School Special

I would have Connor over during and after school while my mom was at work. Once Evan came home to eat lunch on a day we skipped class, the first place I thought of was the shower! We hid their motionless until the reverse noise indicator on the company truck sounded. Whew, that was a close call.

My mom was notorious for backing into the driveway fast in her Aero Van! She burst up on the scene from work after Connor had left one evening and saw a condom wrapper in my trash can. The woman arranged a doctor's appointment for the following day! I got my first pelvic and pap exam; it caused me much discomfort! I didn't particularly appreciate having my legs gapped open and feet in the stirrups at the end of the shortened exam table like the women in momma's pregnancy book. I didn't like sex after that appointment. I even came on my cycle during the process. I was fed up and disgusted! Momma never talked to me about sex, even after that intrusive appointment! Just because I had sex did not mean it was okay to schedule a Pap smear! No one warned me that the doctor would insert a metal object in me and scrap my cervix!!!!!!! That honestly did something to me to this day!

# Now Wait a Minute

Connor's home girls weren't friendly. I was from a different school district; they had to get to know me. The "treat people the way you want to be treated" motto I took pride in expressing would get me beat up showing politeness, and Michelle from The Circle needed to emerge. I was unfamiliar with everyone he said hello to, but best believe the eye rolls once I encountered them alone let me know how they felt.

First semester I made friends in gym class with a young lady named Venus from Connor's neighborhood; she was nice, but I side- eyed her when she came to school wearing shoes I let her borrow for the class. I hate she did this. It was out of order. She caused me to have an unnecessary talk with her. I was too nice if this was how she thanked me for letting her borrow the shoes!!! What impression had I given her to make her assume I wouldn't miss the shoes she had on? I was learning fast that people do things based on their upbringing. It wasn't personal.

A lover of fashion I couldn't help but notice a young lady dressed preppy, rocking my favorite shoes, penny loafers that caught my attention. Her haircut was cute too. Nothing different than when in church or anywhere my eyes captured a mane a synopsis on the hair was concluded; with about two or three more relaxers, her length would be equivalent to "Salt and Pepper's" look in the "Push It" video!

We made eye contact that felt like stare-downs during the 2nd- period class change. I took note of it and her because I'd never given a stranger a look like that, sheesh I wish I hadn't looked; perhaps she knew me or knew of me.

She was being escorted down the hall by a cute guy; I remembered from the activity bus Connor

After describing the young lady named Kenzie and her boo Diamond J, he explained his mom and her mom were friends, and they had known each other since childhood.

Second-semester Health class began, and gym class was over. The room felt like I had walked into a den of lionesses on the 1st day of class. Clueless, I was cordial, although they didn't give the same energy to me they gave Connor. Once I learned their names and his attachment to each lioness, I relaxed until noticing "Michelle Washington is a bitch" written on my desk as I sat down. I started writing back, and it stopped when I wrote, "only someone ugly would say such a thing. Donna looked better than all yawl!" she was the prettier girl in their crew. Boom, it stopped! Just as I figured, the comment would upset an insecure person. That's why I wrote it. Beautiful faces didn't make the person; the heart did; the insult called for a robust response, not praying for my enemies!

# Foods and Nutrition

Omg, Trista from Salem Woods was in the cafeteria during lunch with the professional stare-downer Kenzie. I hadn't seen her since we moved! It turned out she and Kenzie were best friends! I was glad we had the same lunch period. After lunch, we also had Foods and Nutrition together along with Janet.

I was happy for once! We made pizza on Thomas's English muffins. The crust was the best part!

Miss Creekway, Janet, and I hung out during flag practice. Janet and I bonded as cooking partners in this class.

After school, before we started her hair appointment, the first thing we did after we got off the bus was make the cinnamon roll recipe we learned in class. Evan came home to the smells acting like professional caterers dropped off goodies. Without giving him too much, I introduced Janet, and we proceeded to the laundry room to do her beautiful hair. I wasn't her regular stylist, but I knew I could be and hooked her up! Janet had lots of freedom! Her next-door neighbor David was her ride and like a brother to Janet. He graduated from Reynolds the year prior. He was her ride to school, sometimes home, and our ride off campus in the middle of the school day for fun. Highschool was so enjoyable, especially being able to ride around in cars without adults.

My cousin from Thomasville, had her license, and her big sister Kwen let her drive her pretty Honda accord. Cuz drove pretty well as we left family congregated for Sunday dinner in the "Bellview" Community-headed towards the Northside of Winston coincidentally where we pulled up in front of David's house. It's a small world after all popped into my head as I jumped out thrilled to knock on the door and surprise Janet while my cousin and David conversed.

# Good Girls like Bad Boys

Connor didn't meet me after class for the first time. I headed down the steps to the first floor and burst through the heavy double doors leading outside. My feet landed, and before I could start my stride, I stopped in my tracks. To the right of me, Connor, handcuffed, was being escorted by WSPD from the main entrance of the building. Students typically making beelines to 2nd-period class were at a standstill! They could've waited until after the second bell rang, I thought as I watched until the cop car drove off and out of my site. I was an observer like the students wondering what he had done.

Things got very real when I put two and two together; wealthy students from Kent Road and Buena Vista asking me where's Connor all the time made sense now, they wanted weed. His neighborhood female friends from health class may have felt I took him away from their kickbacks. These were customers and friends, not girls that wanted to sleep with him. They bonded with him through the leaf. Not only was he their supplier, he liked to get people high, EXCEPT ME.

The school expelled him! Sadly he was exposed to the game early and didn't want to tell me. Was I supposed to be honored that he's been around me with an illegal substance on him? I hope I wasn't part of the investigation! I had only seen Evan's Top Rolling Papers and smelled the leaf; I hadn't seen it or crumbled herb. Uncle Miles's room smelled like "the leaf." Jada smoked in the living room when she was in town, and Lena's mom kept an incense stick burning in the dining room. It wasn't a biggie, or was it?

During school lunch, I planned to go off campus to visit Connor. I was definitely out of my element! Uncomfortable, I waited in a long line knowing the entire time my mom and Nan would kill me if they knew I was in such a place visiting a drug dealer I loved. I had to be in love in this tiny waiting area only full of people that looked like me. White lawyers were waiting, but white families weren't present, distraught that their loved one was behind bars. Interesting, I thought getting closer to check-in desk.

The wait was over I walked up to the clerk ready to see my man when she asked for the entry required ID that I didn't have. Whelp, what God has for me, it is for me. God had intervened, and I guess that wasn't for me!

# School of Hard Knocks

Connor moved to Carver's District. I was not fond of him attending Carver, especially after BB Jada's best friend's daughter told me he was cheating with a girl named Jerrica! I even reached out to my cousin Cherry who attended the school to see what she knew. I didn't even have my own cousin's number. I found it in the phone book. She had already left for school when I got the bright idea!

# 3 Point Turns

The first semester was over! The driver education course was complete, and after "in-car," I got my permit. I loved to drive! Momma's choir buddy Ms. Patrick was single and adored my sisters and me. She invited us to Sunday school; she lived close by and picked us up. Ms. Patrick was very laid-back, so I asked her to let me drive; I would ride through The Projects past Connor's, although he was sleeping. I went everywhere a licensed driver would allow me! Nan let me drive her gray Cavalier too!

# Train up a Child in the Way They Should Go

Momma and Evan were the GREAT PRETENDERS; surface things like planning a future for me, which I disagreed with, were more important than my mental health. With no input from me, they decided to put "the hairstylist" in a pre-college program called Upward Bound in hopes of me attending college.

Mrs. Addie Hymes from church was the program director! Honey, she and her family; effortlessly turned heads when entering the sanctuary! The daughters rocked natural hairstyles and African garb when relaxers were popular! They were a whole AFRICAN mood! CLASSY and grounded in their roots! These vibes made the program more intriguing. I became okay with attending the program.

The woman got nothing but my respect! I studied her as she spoke with clasped hands—Mrs. Hymes's desire for us to succeed was strong.

At corporate and individual gatherings, she gave harsh but beneficial speeches I'd hide in my heart forever.

My report card analysis reflected her verbally when she said I talk too much the words went deep down in my soul. I agree and was cool that God created me talkative. I did talk a lot, my future job as a hairstylist would require lots of communication.

Meeting Robyn somehow caused me to reflect on my life. Countess Evan's younger sister babysat us both; she was always busy reading books and studying; I talked on the phone and acted like an immature teen. Thankfully things were going UPWARD BOUND!

Since the 1981 wedding, I felt unparented. Upward Bound was right on time; their guidance afforded African American high schoolers a future for GREATNESS! My life path felt meaningful! Aside from religion and my soul-making heaven, no one reflected on the importance of my success on Earth.

# IHOP

Evan purchased a cute White 77 Rabbit with BBS rims. It was a straight drive; he said I could drive it when I got my license. I loved the Volkswagen Golf, Cabriolet, and Scirocco, so he had my undivided attention for once in his life listening to his spill about the car, pretending like all was well "like them" had become part of my character. The man should've been an actor. He was talking and pecking away under the car's hood like the perfect father, excited his daughter was about to start driving. My dumb ass stood there listening as if he hadn't violated me numerous times! How else was I getting a car? Coolie wasn't concerned with my mode of transportation! This was a parental moment I plan to let them have although momma was the only person I wanted to present me with a car! A car wouldn't erase my true feelings toward him.

Speaking of cars, Janet and Trista were both blessed with new vehicles. Trista had a new White Hyundai Excel, and Janet had a Blue Geo Metro hatchback! I was getting around just fine.

# Appropriate Adjustments

I adjusted well to the weekly Upward Bound tutorial sessions; they could keep their summer sessions living on campus. I was not participating! The only thing attractive about staying on campus was being away from Evan. Other than that, summer belonged to Connor and me!

The Upward Bound program gave us a stipend every month to cover transportation. After school, I caught the city bus downtown, where I'd meet Connor. He loved seeing his jeweler AJ at Camel Pawn, who made us personalized pieces with our names, a two-finger ring, and a necklace that spelled out our names. Amongst other things! You had to have a shrimp ring, nugget watch, and HIP-HOP gold chain in that era. Those items were trending! We would also eat, then I'd be off with my bus transfer to tutorial sessions on the WSSU campus that started at 3:45. Sessions ended at 4:45, and we socialized until our parents picked us up, and some took the city bus home.

# Unfamiliar Spirit

Every October, the Classic Fair brought fun to the city of Winston- Salem! My first year in high school US History class came to a halt as the Classic Fair sped by "Society Hill."

With unassembled games and fair rides pulled each student to the window in awe like a magnet.

Saturday night teenagers put on for the city, it seemed the entire school system was there! No way was anybody who thought they were somebody showing up without a new outfit, a fresh shampoo, and barbershop visits!

Optimistic that I had laid eyes on Jerrica, the girl BB said Connor was entertaining; in all the excitement as if a psychic ability manifested, my attention became drawn to this girl that I had never seen and I felt as if I knew.

Driving the "Rabbit" later on that Saturday night off Cleveland Avenue, my observant eyes saw the same girl with a friend we had in common I may have missed at the crowded fair, Chryzaria from the Girls Club. I flagged her down like her tire was flat; she pulled over for me. I said hello to Chryzaria first; knowing Jerrica was the reason I stopped her. Formalities out of the way, I approached the passenger side to say hello to the stranger, and right friendly, she started rolling down the window as I noticed she was even more beautiful up close, and all I could do once it was entirely down was slap her like momma needed to do Evan. Chryzaria skidded off in her black VW Scirocco and left as Jerrica screamed obscenities. I was wrong, but something about her being around my man and possibly twirling on his, "you know what," had me acting like an unfamiliar spirit, took over my body briefly!

That next day was Super Bowl Sunday, my home girl, Yisha, Teeka's friend worked at KFC, so I stopped for a hook-up! Glad I went by there; unbeknownst to me Jerrica was cousins with her good buddy Safari, who heard about the slap and was going to see me on her behalf at school the following day. We weren't besties but we were cool and everyone knew Safari could fight! God used Yisha in a mighty way! I avoided going into the situation blind and dressed appropriately so this "Church Girl" could "BE YE READY"! To fight Safari Monday.

Evan and his game guest ate the chicken. I lost my appetite, learning about the fight the following day.

Retaliation awaited me and I had only been in one fight in 5th grade!?

LaLa my studious friend visiting the weekend of the fair witnessed the slap, and was my voice of reason the night before "the fight." Initially, I made friends with her oldest sister Nina in 2nd grade. Lala and I became close friends in Upward Bound. The sisters were so bright, shame on me for acting like a heathen that Saturday night!

LaLa dated Z. Both Z and Lala were my friends; Z and I were friends 1st as small kids; our families knew each other well, and my loyalty was with him at the end of the day.

I had to keep to myself that Connor slithered out of the Jerrica scenario placing the blame on Z as if he was seeing her. Too many fires would've broken out. As handsome as the opposite sex appeared, It was every man for himself out of the presence of their significant other so at the end of the day, I may have slapped Jerrica for nothing.

Z and Teeka's brother Tim were church boys that matured into tall, fine ball players the girls liked to flock to so nothing surprise me!

Fighting wasn't my cup of tea being prissy was; I provoked this event. I'm sure BDP would buzz with excitement on the way to school!

Monday morning, it was on, and the unavoidable event happened. The fight was over before the first bell rang, and it was a good one. I think us both won! No one ever said I lost, thank God! Had I known they were cousins, I would have thought twice. How honorable it must feel to have someone stand up for you, I thought to myself with profound respect for Safari and a family with such reachable bonds!

# Every Action has a Reaction

Evan put me on punishment after getting a suspension for three days for fighting.

My friend Liz the new girl at school from Bladensburg, M.D. was having a massive sleepover with friends from RJR and North Forsyth for the North vs. Carver football game! Because I was on punishment, I was going to miss it!

It sucked; the fight was the week I had planned for an epic weekend at Liz's! Being friends with creatives was always a blast! What others call extra was self-expression for n my eyes. Liz was full of life, opinionated, and boldly donned wigs, cut with angles, even colored ones! We both were future hairstylists and spent a lot of time at church.

Her mom Mrs. Alexis dazzled with beauty and was very active at St. Seaters Church. Liz was the 90's version of her mom. To my surprise, on my first visit I discovered, she resided across the street from Teeka in the house Teeka's Uncle & Aunt Yandi stayed in and did hair at back in the day. Memories of the good ole days flooded my mind when I stopped by to sit and chat with her in the same basement of the salon I used to get my Jheri Curl done.

Nostalgia set in each time Liz did her signature, pretty DMV-style piggyback roller set on me in the same area of the split-level house as Mrs. Yandi did my Jheri Curl.

Liz transformed the space nicely! Mrs. Alexis had her "Image Within" beauty cream displayed nicely for purchase.

# Lifted Standards

Connor was interested in other people, so I started dibbling and dabbling with a new friend, The Crush; it was a fun match! He could dress and rocked POLO almost every day. I ran into him in school, after school, at football games, and TJ Maxx out shopping. Guys were more relaxed and approaching me since Connor had switched sides of town and schools. I loved how The Crush's extra wavy flat top had me going. Laughing is what we did most; he was silly!

The court system ordered Connor to get a job. He applied and got hired at Casa Guardo. The restaurant was conveniently located in the mall parking lot; I visited the job every time I frequented the mall and would often get greeted by a beautiful WSSU college student, Phyllis, a waitress at the restaurant. Connor spoke of her so often that I thought he had a crush on her. Encountering her so often visiting the job, I could see why Connor liked her so much, and my suspicions were replaced with respect. The advice she gave him concerning me was like a big sister advising her little brother. When he was busy, we chatted. She secretly told me Connor always talked to her about me!

Connor took me on dates there. The fried ice cream was delicious. He had to step up his game after my crazy tail self-slapped Jerrica when he was the person I should've slapped!!!

That Christmas holiday, my gifts got better!

The Beauty did his shopping whenever my birthday or a holiday came, and the lady had HOT taste! Connor had the gifts wrapped. She had me in flavors of suede skirts and sheer floral blouses to match from the hottest store at the mall Contempo Casuals! The cards would have cash inside!

We tried to continue, but the broken trust damaged the relationship. After school before Upward Bound, I began to find Connor sleeping. The deep state of sleep concerned me! I would have to climb up and enter through his second-floor bedroom window for him to be aware I was there. I could tell he wasn't attending school. He was just different.

WSSU Homecoming, being in Upward Bound, put me in a celebratory mood, and it was my first homecoming with a driver's license. Still, I was distracted after the parade, unable to find or reach him by phone. I decided to hunt for him, which angered me as I searched for him in familiar childhood territory in The Circle that was now drug-infested. Walking through my old hood checking for Connor was not as safe as it had been when I walked as a kid.

Magically he soon appeared before I got back to my car. From there, fooling with Connor, we ended up at Jet Way Shopping Center at my favorite place, the salon; It was a clever decoy, the perfect place a guy about to be broken up with can take a soon-to-be ex in hopes of salvaging a relationship or he could also have been trying to keep me from all those cute, testosterone-filled young men I would meet celebrating homecoming.

Once Harvey talked me into a bob cut on my hair I had already slayed for homecoming; I looked so fabulous, momentarily I lost my memory of all he had done!

It wasn't long after I broke off our four-year relationship.

Call me petty, but I associated the connection friends kept with Connor after the split a loyalty barometer. It was equivalent to rewarding him for cheating on me. We all grew apart from that stage because they had things in common that I didn't have with Connor. Knowing the beautiful bonds Janet and I created, to make me jealous, Connor shared that he could've slept with Janet; I was crushed and remembered the song "Self Destruction" playing as he shared the nauseating info with me. From that day forward, songs had a way of reminding me of the excellent and critical times in my life.

# That's What Friends Are For

The Crush came to see me at Miss Creekway's house, we were chilling, and Connor entered uninvited. With a blank stare, and "heat" in hand, talking to both of us. I was unable to make out his words as his lips moved in motion my hearing left. I had only seen stuff like this on television. Connor gave me no decision but to go downstairs with him.

I only participated in his using me because he had a gun.

That summer, we were together for the last time as teens. NWA, aka "Niggers with Attitudes," was the hit album that summer; he perfectly fit the description!

The experience put a wedge between my crush and me; he was not even about that life and should not have been disrespected and so uncomfortable he had to flee!

That day I made a mental note never to introduce friends to my man!

I was too passive to investigate who tipped off Connor about my guest or who omitted to tip me off that he was on the way over. Even if clueless, he was arriving; we broke up; allowing him to enter the house, let alone in the living room where I had a guest, was wrong! I would've never done any shit like that to my guest. I felt betrayed!

The matriarch of the house was at work.

My choice of lodging could've got me a shot while my momma and Evan were out of town.

I couldn't share Connor pulled a gun on me with my momma. I figured it wouldn't matter.

# Window Pains

The temperatures always got warmer and warmer after my birthday! Everybody had come out of hibernation and was outside. Days like this made me want to go out!

The spring season of junior year brought enthusiasm knowing soon I'd be a senior the closer summer got.

I had a license; momma and I didn't hang out as much since I could go wherever I wanted. Out solo shopping, I purchased the cutest floral dress with hot pink Sam and Libby sandals, perfect for my outing to the new teen club "The Zoo."

Evan was at the table when walked in. Yuck! Thanking God his back was to me, I slid past him and to my room; the first room on the right to put on my pajamas. Everyone else was sleeping you could hear a pin drop, so the faint sound at my window in the still of the night caught my attention. To be sure I wasn't bugging, I crept over to the window, then peered out my door, and in my peripheral, momma's door was moving, closing slowly till the doorknob clasp shut. SMH

After digesting it all, I took the long stroll down the hallway knowing no one cared, to knock on momma's door to tell her I heard something at my window; not a soul budged.

It could've been a robber; why wasn't she afraid? Evan, the culprit, had just slid into the bed like a snake, acting asleep when a real man would've checked the property! It was him at the window; Evan knew there was no need to get up to investigate the noise.

This torment had gone unchecked before I developed physically into my late teens.

All I did was be born. I had to depend on my momma for shelter until I turned 18. What the hell did he want with me? Rejection engulfed me like flames, and this man was the root of my pain and need for an escape!

I was fed up with allowing a man to be sexually inappropriate with me repeatedly!

I made her aware he was peeking in my bedroom not too long after that episode; her suggestion to resolve all the peeping was to get dressed in the dark!! Not packing up, heading to Nan's, with plans to file for divorce.

# Scorpion Droppings

It was mentally disturbing observing Evan in action at home then in public grinning and chumming it up with everyone like he doesn't have a predator mode button he clicks on and off.

Momma encouraged the behavior and ignored signs he was unwell.

A mother arriving home to a cracked fish tank with dead fish floating after leaving her daughter in the care of her husband starting dinner messed with my mind. The cinched wall in the kitchen with the iron print I made visible to dinner guests as they ate did not raise eyebrows!

I mustered up strength to tell Nan about Evan's discomforting ways, who responded, "Is it something you did?" I was insulted, even shocked, by my charming Christian grandmother's response!

The dynamic of our relationship changed that day! I took mental note of the statement; it echoed in my head for ions! I can recite where I stood the Saturday I called her. Nan had made me cry for the first time. The pain was worse than my momma's rejection which had become custom. Nan was my mother figure. How could she? For a decade, the adults I blatantly told of Evan's predatory ways had great relationships with him in my face while the blanket of rejection rested on my shoulders. I couldn't name what was happening and was confused! The God Nan introduced me to, who dealt with people who broke the commandments, wasn't dealing with Evan fast enough for me!

# To whom it may concern:

## Psalm 82:3-4

Give justice to the weak and the fatherless; maintain the right of the afflicted and the destitute. Rescue the weak and the needy; deliver them from the hand of the wicked."

# A Wonderful Change

# Has Come Over Me

Junior Year College was the focus. I was more accountable for my actions and understood they impacted my future.

Upward Bound suggested checking over my work to avoid talking when I finished my assignments; each improvement made me proud!

Spring was in the air. My birthday had just passed, April 2, and prom time was near.

My good friend Teeka from 1st grade and I made plans to double-date.

I was happy Teeka was going to Career Center accruing hours in the cosmetology program, so after 3rd period she left campus. I wanted to be there and get my hours in the cosmetology field; I knew I was born a hairstylist! It didn't make sense to me to miss out on that free licensing offered in High school with the opportunity to start my career immediately after graduation! Upward Bound was so college-oriented it considered the industry I loved as "vocational." The students enrolled in the program only attended the Career Center for Advanced Placement classes.

Prom night arrived. We looked gorgeous and knew it! In 1st grade we behaved maturely growing up church girls we were used to sitting still looking pretty in multiple church services with our legs crossed like a lady, reframing from too much childish behavior, which was evident at age seventeen as we dined at the 5-star restaurant parentless that evening in the lovely adult atmosphere.

My Caucasian date, Jodie ordered lamb; it was pretty good when he let me try it. The night ended with a soft peck on the cheek.

Connor clowned me when he found out I was in attendance. I didn't care; Jodie was a gentleman!

We attempted to relight our match; he put his hands on me to the point I told Evan, and they got into a scuffle.

Thankful, but his defending me didn't earn him reward points from me.

# Double-A Batteries

# Aries meets Aquarius

Finally, I met my new boo! My boyfriend Shay and I linked up at Glenn High-Class Day Cookout. I had been seeing him out. His best friend worked with Connor.

Shay was a handsome, terrific dancer with a northern sense of style. Although he was one year older than me, it was my first time dating a spoiled cutie! I was the oldest child and him being the youngest of his siblings, it was easy to notice his mother and sisters spoiled him! He showed me an excellent time and was always a gentleman! He didn't have a car of his own and didn't need one because he had access to many vehicles; in any case, if he didn't, a rental car would be provided by someone!

# Stuck Like Chuck

When I started Upward Bound, I had vowed never to go in the summer, but the time had come; no debating, I went. New boo and all!

The fall program was beneficial; it was ignorant to miss the summer session simply because I preferred to keep up with the regularly scheduled summer I had every year. I was able to escape a family trip to Disney for the same reason when Connor and I dated, but I couldn't get out of Upward Bound's "Summer Session" before my senior year. The summer session lasted six weeks.

Participants had to draw numbers to select roommates; you couldn't share a room with someone you knew! It was like I was a college student, for real! I gained a little weight by eating three big meals a day. Program participants were required to have a glass of milk before they had soda or tea. I told them I was allergic. I couldn't stand milk!

No bickering, jealousy, or hood rat activity ever took place. I can 154 honestly say we all got along well. Dances and field trips to Putt- Putt were all paid for by Upward Bound! Rob Base's "It Takes Two" played the entire summer in our dorm rooms, the dorm hall, in the streets, and at the parties we had!

The summer session was utterly different from the three-day-a-week tutorial sessions offered during the school year. Mrs. Hymes was genius to select teachers that worked in the school system to teach us over the summer. The classes sharpened our skills, we were educated all year, and being prepped for the S.A.T. Test on Saturdays. The parent involvement was AMAZING. The students were very bright; I was honored to have learned amongst them. The end goal for each student to meet the requirements and receive acceptance at the college of their choice had been successful since the 70's when Coolie and my Aunt Zelma were in Upward Bound. Program participants were eligible to enroll at Winston Salem State off the strength of the program was the icing on the cake.

I even took a drama class and was so happy to see my church organist Pete was the drama teacher! I was the Operator in his play called "Wrong Number."

Mrs. Hymes was the GOAT she had an Emmy award-winning group helping her make sure we had all we needed for bright futures!

Life was offering pleasant experiences; THANK GOD!!! Honor roll became a norm. Despite my disgust for Evan, I bet it was because of him, I attended Upward Bound.

# Class of 92

Senior year was here! I missed Trista; she was in college, but luckily, her mom Mrs. Zella had become my first mobile client. Running into Trista before her and her cute boyfriend, Tim, headed back to NCCU in Durham was always the mood when I arrived for the Sunday appointment. I was able to see the items she purchased from the mall over the weekend.

I shouldn't compare, but Trista's mom Mrs. Zella lived well without a husband. Jazz played in the background, a nice soft incense smell or aroma of food hit you as you walked in and the house was spotless! She seemed content with dating, traveling, caring for her son, and putting Trista through college. Momma was missing out she was so pretty and deserved to live her best life!

Being a senior on campus was so refreshing!

Cassidy was a pleasant surprise senior year. Ya girl moved to Reynolds school district; we picked right up from when we met at

Kennedy Middle School.

I gravitated away from my friendship with LaLa; it tapered off once she was no longer in Upward Bound. I didn't see her that much since she took classes at the Career Center; we rarely saw each other. She was expecting a bundle of joy.

Yisha road to school with me during senior year! We laughed all the way there! She would say her face was melting because I kept the heat on high! Yisha was a tall beautiful mahogany brown girl with ultra-thick hair I had a vision for but she was Teeka's client so I left well enough alone. She was such a boy-crazed girl! I was so used to Kenzie and Trista but she and Yisha were real cool they had classes together.

Cassidy was the perfect addition to our lunch table. We all were bright and fashionable!

The "Juice Crew" is what we named ourselves. The first booth belonged to us; we decorated when we observed birthdays and shared tasty foods.

It was all good until the cat was out of the bag! Kenzie and Yisha kept called "Nas" at the lunch table. The guy turned out to be Cassidy 's boyfriend, Darius! All my friends were in relationships; questioning the authenticity of the names of their boyfriends was unnecessary, I thought.

Trista was my only connection to the young lady.

I was saddened to discover how naive Cassidy and I were. We seriously were silly church girls going through puberty. We were in the presence of a girl with no curfew, and way more freedom!

One thing about Yisha was she had no shame in her game, which she sincerely shared, if it were her seeing Darius I would not have been surprised. During the ride to school together daily, various subjects arose but not this!

Not communicating with LaLa and coming to grips she was no angel I settled in with the knowledge Yisha and Z were "buddies!" LaLa was "buddies" with his confidant.

Kenzie; however, caught me off guard but I knew she had it in her from her unwarranted stare-down freshman year.

Darius was Trista's cousin; she and Kenzie were like sisters; they did everything together. Darius smirked a lot but was very attractive. His tented reddish brown, naturally curly hair, and freckles made him unique. Perhaps in proximity to him over the years naturally an attraction arose and then innocently, one hot summer day buzzed up during a visit, BAM DARIUS got a whole name change!!!!

Unaware of what a buzz felt like, who knows what took place? Cassidy and I were on natural highs. My attempt at smoking failed freshman year in David's car. Everyone cheered when I finally gave it a try but when I could not get the smoke to blow through my nostrils I gave up trying.

# I COULD GET USED TO THIS

Luckily since I was smart enough to make known college was a waste for a cosmetologist, I was the perfect selection for the pilot program W.I.S.E thru Wachovia, which stood for Wachovia's Involvement in Student Education within the Upward Bound program. Age was a nonreactor.

Participants became permanent part-time employees on the strength of being Upward Bound participants; they didn't even interview us!

After school, I reported to the bank's West End Center on days I did not have tutorial sessions. Departments offered participants full-time hours in the summer. The benefits were endless!

The opportunity afforded us to do something never heard of in the history of Upward Bound, attend Forsyth Technical Community, a two- year College instead of attending a four-year college!!! Receiving my associate's degree early advanced my plan to go to beauty school earlier!

It was settled I'd get an Associate's Degree in Banking and Finance after graduation! Once your two-year course of studies was complete, you became a permanent full-time employee!

Working for Wachovia meant a lot in my city, especially since I was so young in the corporate world. I worked full-time in the summer and ten hours a week during the school year.

Accumulating the hours would also look great on my leasing application for my apartment after graduation.

I liked dressing up and acting like an adult, so the professional dress code required would not be a problem.

The workplace was entertaining; I noticed as we toured the company! The highlight was meeting Mr. Baker, who at that time was President of Wachovia Bank, and his right-hand lady Mrs. Lynn, a sharp sister who exuded properness and was our contact person over the W.I.S.E. Program.

Information Systems is the department I reported to; my liaison was Karen.

Pickup and delivery of Inner and Outer office mail were my responsibilities. Daily I made two trips on the trolley to the Phillips Building, where momma worked in the Retail Loan department of Wachovia. Although she never told me, she had to be proud of me. We both worked at the bank and I always wanted to be like her as a kid!

# 1st Time Buyer

My momma and Evan took me to get a car through a first-time buyers program at the Ford dealership. They co-signed on my new 1992 four- door strawberry red Ford Escort Sedan. I was grateful for a new car and the signature. From the outside looking in it appeared they got their teenage daughter a new car, LOL! Don't get me wrong; I was cute when I pulled up but the assumption they paid the note just because I was a high schooler was bs! Indeed it was customary for parents to foot the bill however we were not dealing with ordinary parents. Momma and Evan had me give them money towards the water bill so NOPE, they parented differently. If unbelievable was a couple it was them!

Everyone thought we were rich, the gag is, those Wachovia checks and hair money covered the $210 payment and $118 for car insurance.

Although I got myself into debt, to process the blessing I viewed 162 the new bill as an opportunity to build my credit! My appreciation for my first whip should've been based on pure joy, I was so clouded in happy times like this knowing when people show you who they are believe them. I certainly had come to know who Evan was, and I believed he was manipulative! That nigga must've had some powerful pillow talk. You see, I laid my pretty head on pillows listening to Connor drip lies and sweet honey only to find out the word on the streets was he allowed people to view and snort coke off pics I let him take of me. Thanks to Evan, mimicking the scantily clad pics I viewed as a child from his porn magazine collection made the photoshoot child's play.

Momma set the tone for his treatment towards us the first time he violated me and it went unchecked! He got cockier the older I got.

One day God would remove the scales from momma's eyes.

# Bonnie and Clyde

Yassssss, I was home alone, I had the house all to myself. Momma and Evan were in the Bahamas!

The phone rang, and the caller stated Ford Motor Credit was calling about my car payment. I was informed it was two months behind. The money was given to momma, whom I trusted mailed the payments. I thought it was Shay prank calling, so I asked the male on the line to hang up and call back. They did, and it indeed was the finance company on the line.

When momma returned I ran it by momma, who advised, "the best thing for you to do is send the payments yourself!" That wasn't a problem had she updated me to do so in advance!

I was nineteen and recognized this unacceptable attitude very well from her! Sending off the payment wasn't going to catch up with the behind payments.

Evan was smart and aware he was in a union with a woman from a bloodline of meek and mild women.

He had grouped me with them, making me an easy target, no one was protecting or rescuing me!

Shit was bout to change! No disrespect I refused to participate in these cycles with momma and Evan! One minute we up, then down. Their ability to snap back like nothing ever happened was driving me nuts!

Taking care of personal business on the clock was unusual for me but the insurance company informed me of how insurance worked and told me the end of each policy; the company refunded checks based on your account activity before each renewal. Evan kept the last check they mailed me. He also had me pay insurance monthly when five payments covered the 6-month policy!!

Digesting they went on vacation with extra spending money that includes my car payment and insurance refund check had me burning inside!

I didn't give a dam my three colleagues sat in the quad an earshot away as I dialed momma; who repeatedly hung up!

My liaison allowed me to take a break to pull it together. Tears streamed down my cheeks as I mentally struggled with how she could treat her child this way!

I hopped on the first company Trolley to momma's job.

When I arrived, as if she knew I was on my way I entered the lobby as she exited through the doors; like she hadn't seen me.

On the trolley ride over with everything in me, I intended to conduct myself professionally. Rejection didn't give a dam after she ignored me. I blurted out, "how could you stand by and let this man do what he wanted?!!!!!"

Beautiful as momma was, my truth embarrassed her, poised and head held high she stayed mute. As if she had never met me, momma headed across the street to escape me, her firstborn child. I could've kept after her, but something stopped me in my tracks as I watched her head around a corner and disappeared from my sight. I wasn't going to embarrass myself chasing her while observers saw it all play out!

My mind changed that day! I no longer wanted to be like my momma!

The things occurring were taking a toll on me. The scripture "The devil came to kill, steal, and destroy," came to my mind. My concerns were sincere. Communication was not a strength of mommas! It didn't have to be like this; all I wanted was my account paid current, a reimbursement for the months I overpaid my car insurance, and the refund check mailed to me at the end of the policy!

On the ride back to the West End Center, with my adult bank badge, I was utterly DISGUSTED with the ways of the mother God gave me!

# WISE Girl

W.I.S.E. pilot program became a genuine partnership with Upward Bound! Once the association became permanent, I was transferred from Information Systems to the Student Financial Services department.

My duties consisted of mail pick-ups three times daily, and I stuffed and folded deferments.

Saturdays, the department offered overtime hours, 8 am to 12 pm. The department wasn't as intense as the weekly hustle and bustle of Monday through Friday; no supervisors worked on the weekends. We assembled in the conference room at the enormous table, stuffing and folding deferments and forbearances. At the same time, they had adult conversations, and of course, I was all ears and adding things that may be useful later to my long-term memory bank. The adults I worked with hung out the night before and still had alcoholic beverages in their systems. They were very laid back. I found out what a hangover was, lol! Doughnuts with coffee and pizza were a great perk to get me there.

# Charlie's Angels

## Angel 1

Sheena, my mentor, was born and raised in New York. I liked my liaison in the pilot phase of W.I.S.E., but witnessing her turn her churchy ways switch on and off made me question her authenticity.

Sheena had a brilliant way of thinking! Out the gate, we had so much fun sometimes that I forgot I was at work! During training, I admired how she transformed the mail pickup route into a social hour. I tagged along with her and her friends for the afternoon break after school. On days when school was out, I looked forward to the two twenty-minute and one-hour lunch breaks.

Sex came up a lot. I was all ears as I enjoyed my food! Tevin from the "Forms" department of Student Financial Services, whom women at the table labeled "a freak," spoke inappropriately around me regardless of my age.

Over time Sheena and I got close! On my first trip accompanying her to the mall, she admonished me to "get whatever you want!" I graciously picked out some bomb tights with a psychedelic print and a lime green shirt that fell just over my buttocks and I even got black booties! God knows I needed an environment I felt comfortable. After visiting her luxurious apartment several times and frequenting the pool, she showed me where the spare key was.

One day I arrived at the office, and Sheena came in late.

During lunch, we headed to the parking lot, her Ford Escort was nowhere to be found as she approached a brand new, fully loaded white Celica and unlocked the door; sharing she had just left the dealership once we were nestled in.

After work, that evening chilling at Sheena's, like a fairy God angel she asked "you want to drive my car?" I said yes and next thing you know shawty was headed up Silas Creek to Jonestown Road. Back at the house Momma and Evan didn't ask any questions when I pulled up to shower and dress for the Reynolds vs. Mount Tabor game.

All that power under the hood had me on cloud nine driving the Celica! Riding solo that Friday night to a big rivalry football game!

After the game she let me keep the new car overnight; when I went to give it back, she let me know the key to her Escort GT was in the car under the mat and that the dealer wouldn't be back to the lot until Monday if I wanted to drive it. With pleasure, I drove the wheels off and returned the vehicle late that Sunday night. GOD was SO GOOD!

# Angel 2

Mia Sheena's friend got her hair done regularly! My confidence in hair expanded when she took me to Beauty World and purchased everything I needed to do my clients' hair.

The gold jewelry and bangles she donned decorated her arms like a princess making her long nails stand out! Soon Mia got a new white 1991 Jetta with a professionally installed mobile phone that, during that time, was a luxury most doctors had!!! It was a nice upgrade. I planned on getting one someday.

My Home girl RIA and I made a pit stop by Mia's one Sunday afternoon. Her shoe closet held hundreds of pairs of shoes and designer perfumes lined the dresser top!

Mia had guy friends that did whatever she asked. I was taking notes.

Once, Mia realized we were headed to The Lake where she used to hang out, no shade to my 92 strawberry red Escort Sedan she just knew the vibes and offered to let me push her whip, and I utterly enjoyed showing off!

We stunted in the Jetta, cruising all up and through East Winston, driving the car of my dreams!

The gesture was something a big sister granted her teenage sister, and I appreciated her kindness!

# Angel 3

Paula was like family to Mia. Ultra-pretty, prim and professional, and she knew it!! Her appearance stayed on point.

I'd sit in her cubicle and talk to her about whatever; she never pushed me away because she was "on the clock" Plus, I'm sure I made the time pass. She taught me to glue in hair weaves for volume after becoming a faithful client. Paula was the 3rd generation of superb cooks! I ate some of the best food ever at her house, and I fell in love with her Mom, Grandma, and Papa once she introduced us. The Cods had an open door for me permanently after my initial visit, and I instantly became glued to her entire family, that became clients as well. I went there after work and Upward Bound instead of home many days and stayed close to bedtime watching Paula love and raise her son Tate; he was so spoiled! They were enriching him in love; he had everything a little boy could conceive.

I love my family, but exposure to Paula's family made me aware I how neglected I had been. I believe God wanted me to see a different family dynamic. The family nucleus was tight; Momma would've been embarrassed to continue in a marriage with the man she married if she were a part of this family!!! They raised hell over theirs!!! Funeral arrangements would've been completed the first time he touched my bedroom door knob! Paula was the best! Out of nowhere, I now had big sisters that cared about me, not just a job. All three of them were angels in disguise God connected me with to be beautiful and gracious to me!

# Approved

Mia was graduating from college. I was about to graduate high school when she started apartment hunting. I was honored when she invited me to roommate with her! I applied but didn't think much about it again till Evan stated, "I didn't know you were moving out," as he passed me the envelope with the apartment logo containing my approval letter. Attempting to interact with me friendly. Those perve vibes were always present, so I didn't respond and stayed to myself until momma was home. I exhaled and laid back on my water bed; it felt good to know that I could fly the coop someday and do things like getting dressed with the lights on, with no worries or the terror of being watched unknowingly. I knew I was leaving as soon as I graduated, thanks to EVAN!

# Premature Maturity

Senior prom Shay and I stayed out all night. Somebody got him a hotel room.

Aside from being a flower girl, it had been a minute since I had gotten formally dressed. Abraham gave me a gorgeous up do with rhinestones! Nan was the queen of makeup, after watching her and momma I put my makeup skills to work.

Prom night was spiffy! The Quail Downtown Winston located at the Adams Mark is where we dined, the prom was within walking distance. Shay and I wore black and white.

The Residence Inn hotel room was all ours afterward!! I enjoyed looking out the window wearing my first lingerie purchase I made especially for that evening. The two-piece purple satin set reminded me of an "indoor" short set, it fit loosely on my skinny body but it was really cute. Mama did my laundry, if my lingerie collection was going to expand I needed to move as soon as graduation was over!

Spring temperatures were a reminder it was almost summer; the heat made me look forward to "Senior Beach Week" after graduation. The graduation ceremony was a blur, but I did it!!! Cheering took place when the principal called my name. Hearing the distinctness of momma's voice yell out is how I imagined that day all my life but,

I appreciate the noise made for me.

Exiting the stage, some attendees got as close as possible to capture the graduates. Camera flashes flickered like crazy!

My high school alums graciously exited the prestigious auditorium aisle past the roaring audience as instructed at rehearsal earlier that morning. Groups waited patiently with balloons and flowers and positioned themselves in the lobby eager to grab their grad's attention.

God or angels guided me out the door to the right towards those celebrating, and the first face I saw was one I don't see often; Coolie, to my surprise! This miracle caused me to feel celebrated by his mere presence! Coolie showing up there, sober on a Friday evening was priceless.

Evan, the photographer, to my dismay, did not have his camera bag with him. Dam him when I needed him to act step fatherly; he didn't.

Let me find out my accomplishment made him feel some type of way because his ass dropped out of Reynolds and got his G.E.D.! My cap and gown photo taken at school was the only picture to remind me of that sea of white on the stage that evening. Aside from the  professional cap and gown photos cropped from the chest up taken through the school, once I pondered on it I realized no photos of momma's graduation day existed either.

Back at the house after I changed momma came into my room to present me with a crisp $100 bill. It was perfect timing, I got her to capture a memory of that day in my outfit with my disposable camera I used for hair. No monkey could stop my show!

Then I was off to "Project Graduation," the citywide celebration for all the Winston Salem Forsyth County School System graduates held at the fairgrounds! Shay and I went to Charlotte for a week instead of Beach Week the following morning. That week on my own was exhilarating!

# My Block

I got my place after graduation like I said I would. I didn't ask if I could move; I simply told momma I had my apartment keys. Momma and Evan popped up at my place like "The Huxtables" after I moved out one Sunday afternoon. My dumb ass welcomed them in like parents who assisted in my move. My bed looked like two people slept there. Evan went one way, and momma opened every empty kitchen cabinet and even checked the lower cabinets like Shay was hiding underneath. Startled by their unannounced arrival, I asked him to jump off the second-floor balcony when they knocked. That was a dangerous request! Watching these two look around my one-bedroom was hilarious because I was too wet behind the ears to demand they sit the hell down! Momma did not open her door if she did not know you were coming but did a pop-up on me. Guest came in and sat down when visiting a person's home; unfortunately, I allowed them to run amuck. The fake family production residue was still on me, so I participated like a young Christian whose "concerned parents" had come to visit and see their child's new apartment; the pop-up visit made me anxious! Common sense didn't tell momma she should have come alone, and this was a survival mode move to get away from her husband.

How they mustered up the strength to roll up like I was busted and they could still control me after I moved away from them was wild!!!

Unfortunately, they didn't compliment my place or take a seat on the new leather chairs I financed. Once they finished being nosey, with no concern for my empty cabinets they departed in less than 10 minutes like dysfunctional royal families do after scoping out how I lived. The underserved respect I gave them wasn't enough that was the last time I would allow them to walk over me!

# Call Tyrone

The babysitters club was closed, I was no longer babysitting Emily and Brooklyn anymore, but Shay's presence felt like I had a son. I felt uncomfortable paying all the bills with him there and wasn't sure how to get out of the snare. We OD'd on Steakums, fries, and soda. It had been a while since I had a good meal with green vegetables.

LOUD Arguments arose whenever I questioned Shay about bill money! Insanity had me leave my own house mad, to get peace. He was my man, not a joint partner on my lease! Embarrassed, I bet the neighbors assumed we moved in together; the lines blurred! That mouth on him would make one think I was at his house; he was there more than me and had his cousin and friends over to smoke and play the game. There was too much dip on his chip! It was a "one" bedroom, for crying out loud!! I felt trapped in my place. I grew up in well-preserved living rooms only sat in when guests visited. Chummy talk and laughter filled the room with folk sitting with their legs crossed at the ankle or knee in what was considered the nicest room in the house. My plans to keep that tradition were failing horribly with my unwanted roomie who knew better because his mom had a humongous house and storage filled with nice furniture?

Shay lost that, work steady job energy he had when I lived with momma but stayed stocked with his smokes and stuff.

Foolishly I thought of loaning Shay my car while I was at work to look for a job I was so desperate. Working wasn't a problem for him, the dire need for permanent employment and understanding his paychecks couldn't just cover fun was my prayer!

Car on hand he could be readily available to interview. I just had one easy request, "NO SMOKING" inside the car.

It was evident someone with long legs, most likely his cousin had been in the passenger seat I had to readjust when he picked me up from work. Fresh off the clock I let it go and preserved my energy.

The car smelled like cigarettes one day he arrived; you would think a person breaking the rules would surprise the owner with a car washed and vacuumed with air fresheners dangling! Shay didn't consider airing out the vehicle or spraying cologne to mask the odor. Arguing he hadn't smoked in the car was more favorable until I turned to my left and saw a cigarette butt that burned into the seat cushion; when I grabbed the cigarette, cool ash fell, and a hole the size of the filter was visible. The cigarette flew back into the car after he flipped it out the window. The proof he smoked after arguing with me up and down he had not smoked angered him! My freaking seat was damaged; if anyone needed to be mad, it was me.

Regardless of how much I loved Shay, if he could not contribute, he definitely couldn't stay every night or control me! It was weighing down the new furniture and ruining our relationship.

# True Colors Shining Through

My little sisters and I hung out for the day; it was getting late, and the pizza we ordered was taking forever to arrive, so I called to tell them, but I asked if they could stay overnight. Evan would not let my little sisters spend the night and told me to bring them home, which was less than 4 minutes away. It's funny how the same predator with access to me 365 days a year wouldn't let them stay one night at my place. Daddy or not they were better off with me if they knew what I knew! Going back and forth with Evan was a waste! I gave in, but I didn't budge till after 1 a.m.!!!!! My sisters were all confused about why they couldn't stay.

On the drive back to my apartment from momma's, 19-year-olds with mentally sane parents listened to music as loud as it would go, unlike "them" I, zoned in on the dam nerve of them not allowing the girls to stay the night!

Those summers alone babysitting. They saved tremendously in daycare costs for two children! Was it that deep to keep us from enjoying our pizza and bonding as sisters? Momma made me feel used! Had my ass held hostage with the girls and a list of things to clean, she even washed uber loads of laundry and the wet clothes for me to hang out on the line and bring inside then separate after they dried! Thank God for teaching me how to run a household but I was unable to go out and play or have friends over until they were off work!

I respected my mom and had to do what she told me, but I realized that moment I was the slave of the family she and Evan used like stepchildren often are.

A teenager's Saturday nights out with friends shouldn't have revolved around combing hair the morning of church. She was waking me before my alarm went off like I birthed children and didn't need time to dress myself. The same went for her hair; without warning, she would just up and shampoo it regardless of my plans; I "had" to curl it, period. I enjoyed time in the mirror before hanging with friends, but she didn't care if I had plans!

Parents made demands and used the church's favorite threat to a child. Ephesians 6:2, "Honor thy father and mother or your days may be shortened," omitting acknowledgment of their behaviors that "GREATLY PROVOKED" offspring! Our mother-daughter dynamic was unimaginable.

# Locked Out

I stopped by mommas periodically; regardless if anyone was home, sometimes on the way out, I took toilet tissue, a stick of butter, depending on what I was cooking, and small things to my place until one day my key wouldn't fit. Evan ass changed the locks!!! Locked out, I rang the bell at the front door, before they could open the door all the way I decided THAT WAS THE DAY to let it all hang out, and commenced to cursing them out like DOGS on the front porch right there not caring Emily and Brooklyn were in attendance. The desire left my body to ever return after that! Of course, they looked at me like "I" was out of control but didn't give a dam the understanding they were under Evan's spell and were inconsiderate of my feelings WHEN THEY NEEDED TO FOCUS THE LENS ON HIM!

My sisters meant the world to me but Evan and momma set the narrative of everything, no telling what lies they told them after I left.

As much as I hated it, taking my sisters' places, purchasing outfits for them, going to eat pizza, and making rice-crispy marshmallow treats would have to cease.

Shay was always present even though he had it made rent-free at his Uncle's pad. I had no one else, so it was fine! Dropping me off at work got old, especially after he started picking me up late.

Working to pay rent, utilities, car payments, and car insurance independently as a teenager was a huge financial responsibility. Fingers pointed back at Evan!! THAT NIGGA was NO REASON FOR ME TO STRUGGLE FINANCIALLY!!! Unfortunately, I had to break the lease and move back home "briefly," Evan had changed those locks for nothing! SUCKA!

# What the Hell is Going On

One chill, rainy Saturday afternoon, I had just laid back on the bed after getting the mail and jumped up after hearing yelling in the hallway; when I made it out of my room and headed towards the voices coming from the den, momma was on Evan's heels, intensely grasping at mail-in Evan's hand that he refused to give to her! Momma was about out of her robe clawing at his arm to grasp the envelope he held high in the air out of her reach! I could've helped, but left her to her own devices as she had done when Evan showed me sides he hid from others. Like a block of ice, frozen, I watched helplessly. Momma finally snatched the envelope that ripped during the pull revealing a black-and-white photo of this light-skinned lady with a pretty roller set like Dorothy Dandridge. WOW, if she went up against Evan the first time he entered my room and fought for me as she did for that piece of mail where would I be? Where would we be?

I still couldn't figure out why the hell she was still with the nigga?????

# A Sick Individual

Moving was always at the forefront; I was going to make the most of it financially while I was there.

It was nothing for me to shower after doing clients' hair before hanging out with my friends.

One beautiful summer Saturday, after showering, sunlight shined through the floor vent!!!! Quickly I threw something on, yelling for momma, who caught up with me in the front yard.

The crawlspace door was open. We entered, it was my first time under the house standing on the foundation able to visually see the layout of the home on the broom-swept floor, void of dirt, dust, and spider webs unlike under the old house.

"This man was sneaky," I thought to myself looking around at the clean area that could've been slept in during spring and summer months.

My bathroom vent was the only one with distinct streaking light from the interior of the house shining through the ample space underneath the house directing attention to my bathroom! Discovering he had watched me towel off defeated me. Knowing winters, I welcomed the warmth that flowed from the booby-trapped vent made me BOIL!!!

The mystery of where the sunlight came from was resolved but Evan was still nowhere to be found as Momma yelled his name. There was no response. I think he knew the layout under the house so well he hid, looking at us.

On my own briefly, I forgot that quickly; I was amongst a predator. Evan had been invading my privacy for ages, this was taking shit to new heights. Bathing at Momma's house just wasn't safe; no telling how long since the purchase of the home the freak had watched me exposed nude exiting the shower before I obtained my apartment!!!!

The man knows I love the heat. As a kid, the bottom of one of my feet would be planted on the square vent like a shoe while the heat-blasted out the vent as I watched television.

Discovering the views through my vent under the house where I stood to towel off defeated me. Thoughts of cold mornings, I welcomed the warmth that flowed from the vent made me BOIL!!!

I WISH THIS WAS MADE UP but, headed back around to the side entrance of the house scanning the property for Evan, visible "MALE" footprints in momma's flowerbed were before our eyes! Someone seemingly stepped off the edge of the porch leaving footprints feet from my bathroom window in momma's lovely flowerbed!! It was NOT a male deer either; it was someone in a haste with work boots about Evan size. The same path anyone with good sense and eyesight took that placed them on the porch, steps from the front door of the house is the only path to exit the porch properly.

I'm not a cop but the footprints appeared someone, jetted and said f them flowers.

This guy was a maniac! Suppose the neighbors saw him peeking in the window regardless of which window he was peeking in. Momma and the girls bathed in there. He was weird, but why spy on the woman you slept in the bed with?

Somebody had piqued interest in someone behind those windows.

The front yard was too huge for a "peeping Tom" to risk being caught walking up on and or escaping the property!

Momma's resolve for the sun shining through was to tell his daddy!? Woooooooow, I thought to myself, let's see if this remnant works better than her recommendation for me to get dressed in the dark; which was an epic failure, by the way, Evan assumed he was amongst fools, after momma soft threats some mysterious stranger was at my window right before Evan went to sleep could be heard until he went to bed!

I learned about mini blinds that night. Taking a good look with the light on in my room I ensure they were turned the appropriate way so no one could see inside!

Moving was a priority!

The vent stayed closed! Towels covered the vent in my room. Paranoid, anxious thoughts visited me like at the old house during my shower I took in momma's room.

My new routine involved taking my clothes inside the bathroom to avoid dressing in the dark. Knowing how crafty Evan was; my last option was my clothes closet which involved being exposed once I pulled the shower curtain back or walked into my room, so drying off and dressing in the tub was the only place left and the only place I felt I had privacy. Unaware that the viewing as extensive as it was, someday when I had a child if things did not work out between the father and the only way

stepdad would work is  if my child was grown and on their own.
!!!!!

# Hanging On Like Spit and Bubblegum

Shay and I were still hanging in there, skating on thin ice. I was doing hair and received a call; "my high school buddies, Yisha and Kenzie, were rode thru the club in Shay's rental car the night prior as I slept the night away unaware. Yisha didn't even like to club! Next, the caller explained she and Shay's cousin were kicking it! Chile I clicked off that call so fast and called him! I needed answers immediately but got no answer!!! Shay failing to mention they were dating was going to make me simultaneously click the ESC, ALT, and DELETE buttons on him! The only reason Cassidy and I were not speaking to them is that Yisha sided with Kenzie after the "illegal name change."

I wasn't even aware Kenzie was home for the summer from college; we hadn't kept in contact or spoken since the revelation of Nas. She and Kenzie did everything together before graduation and so did Shay and his cousin.

I had a reason not to trust men and a reason not to trust them chics!

I hooked his cousin up with Janet. It was a cohesive effort between Shay and me. However, this tattered on sneakiness!

My presence was needed if carpooling, smoking, or drinking, took place!!! It was clear Yisha and Kenzie might "try it" with ya, man!

If capable of doing that to a friend, a dam certainly would not be given if she wasn't in contact with the person.

I was MAD!!!!! Shay and I spoke after I finished my clients. Tell me what was up is all he had to do. He finally admitted they all looked at a movie.

Petty, I was going to the club too later that night and he couldn't stop SHIT!

Livid, I took a shower and changed my clothes, picked up my girl Cassidy and did a drive-by Kenzie's house. I stepped up to the full porch and threatened "it's on if I find out you f'd Shay," and left!

When I lose trust in a person, I lose respect for the person. The broken trust permitted me to break a rule! I no longer trusted Shay! I couldn't change who his cousin was dating, but I could change who I dated.

Having a random conversation with Shay one day, Yisha yelled, "come on, Kenzie," I thought to myself, I know this boy wasn't with Yisha. Cassidy and I were eating in the area near both of their apartments. I caught up with him in front of the seafood restaurant and slammed him! Yisha ass was next on the list because after doing all that, I found out Kenzie wasn't even with her! The devil knew saying that would trigger me, and it did!!!

Later that night, in BDP I ran into her at the phone booth near the Game Room and confronted her about the situation. We got into a fight; her shirt was off when I finished with her!

# Is This The End

The Black Spring Festival in Atlanta was coming, and I planned to attend! Hopeful I'd meet a new guy; excitement overflowed shopping for outfits with the money I should've saved for my move. Momma promised to pay for the hair appointment I scheduled.

On the day of my appointment, she said didn't have cash on her and told me that she would pay me back before I left. On the morning of the trip, I explained I would be gone when she got off and needed the money, and she proceeded to tell me Evan said no! Of all the things to say!!! What angered me is she could've made me aware of this when she found out, but I wasn't important enough.

I had heard this my entire life, and I was sick of it! Updating me that something changed would've been nice.

"He ain't my daddy!!!" I yelled. "That peeping Tom!" "Going to church with porn in his closet," I announced. "Evan a pervert and a cheater!" I blurted. Hitting me didn't keep me from refreshing her memory that she hadn't protected me!

"Shut up!" she shouted repeatedly as she beat me with a broom in front of my sisters for shouting things I had held inside since early childhood when using her hands was null in void. Momma COULD NOT shut me up!!!!!!!

I called Nan and made her aware of the ordeal, and she advised me to come to see her before I left and gave me money!

# First Time in the A

The streets of Atlanta, G.A., were jammed packed! Although momma beat the hell out of me that morning, on Georgia pavement I stood with colleges I had dreamed of visiting in view! The infamous Spelman College Campus was super prestigious for black girls to attend.

Young adults were all over the place dressed scantily. We walked for miles on a natural high yelling out the name of states on car tags from places in the United States that had driven distances that shocked us. Our drive was 4 1/2 hours; I'm sure the group in the vehicle with Alaska tags had gone for days. Some had traveled from places I didn't know black people lived.

Strolling in Buckhead landed us at Lennox Mall. Cars could barely get by as we made our way through the busy traffic. A white Lady in protest of the "Freaknik" visitors captivated me as she yelled the Word of God! The sleeves of her clothing were the only garments on her exposed. A massive two-sided sign shielding her entire body to the ground with scripture written on it ended with Jesus Saves in bold print, held by straps resting on her shoulders. The lady fit the term I heard called "SOLD OUT," I considered her sold out for God for sure! I like radicals because they had ways of capturing your attention with their message! The lady was bold! I was clueless that someday I, too, would have a radical cause to fight for.

In G.A. I ran into the owners of Prime Time, a venue the people from my city frequented. Representing in a limousine, which was dope especially if you wanted to drink and ride and a sign of wealth in the '90s, girls were on them like bees on honey.

Everyone was different, respectfully and no one could judge anyone at a festival with the name "Freaknik" whether you were freaky or not. I wasn't there "yet" but learning quickly at this festival how to get expenses paid.

The guys had game, some had money with flashy cars, women dressed sexy and the attendees were intoxicated.

Everyone was friendly. I had so many phone numbers written down in my pockets from guys I met! Music blaring attracted groups of dancers to cars with huge speakers in the trunk!

We wanted to go to the Underground. It had shops and this famous nail spot that specialized in airbrushed nails everyone from Winston buzzed about and wanted to visit, but Interstate 85 came to a halt!

The FREAKNIK festival had spilled onto the highway! Car drivers and riders were out of their cars and walking on the highway. If drones had captured photos in 1995, it would've appeared ants invaded the city!

A male of small stature was approaching cars still occupied in the lanes, screams roared from each vehicle he approached; once he came to us, we found out why they screamed so loud! The gentleman held a picture that showed his private parts. Lol; for $1, you could see in the flesh! According to that picture, he had a "mass weapon of destruction," but I was NOT participating!

Sunday Piedmont Park is where everybody was going to be according to flyers and new friends we met. We should've been heading back to N.C. that morning.

The park looked like Black Woodstock.

I'd never been around this many black people. Nan would've been so mad at me; I was braless in this white Billion Dollar Babe TSHIRT, short shorts with calf-length boots! I promise I wasn't a threat at all. The carload of naked girls draped in sheets that flashed the crowd shut it down! Men were running after the car for blocks!

The MTV Mobile Bus was live. I walked on the bus! I never wanted that weekend to end!

The festival was national, and as I intended, I met a lot of guys, my connection was with a guy named Peace from New York. We frequently spoke on the phone after the trip.

# Welcome to the Terror Zone

The first thing I did, like any good daughter, despite Friday's Broom Beating, was let momma know I made it home safely. With seriousness in her voice, she instructed me to remain in my room when Evan got home and not to say anything to him. As usual, I did as she told me. Evan, however, didn't get the memo or possibly didn't give a dam because he knocked on my door, clueless that I was on my private line with Nan stating "I want to talk to you!" With pride I can ignore him, momma had already told me what was up. "Do you hear me?!" he asked as I ignored him. I remained silent; without asking am I dressed; noises from him fumbling with the lock started as the expert locksmith unlocked the door. Repeating, "I want to talk to you" in the living room he looked do upset I just followed behind him. The living room; oddly made me assume he would act civilized.

He opened with, "You're going to pay for everything you said in front of the girls and your momma!" My brow raised as I listened to his rant. He explained I had to start going to Sunday school. I couldn't say Dam Sunday School but those were my exact thoughts, his ass needed to "pay" for his failed attempts at baiting me over 15 years! Being kind, "I will not," was my response as I walked out of the living room picking up speed down the long hallway towards my room to lock the door again, as he came charging after me! Grabbing the phone on the wall in the kitchen I dialed Nan faster than I ever had, and he ripped the receiver from my hand and started stomping and assaulting me till I escaped and exited the house barefoot. I ran to the neighbors asking hysterically to use the phone! With sobs, I called momma and Mia. I stood in the neighbor's doorway after the calls and waited for them and walked towards the house after Nan drove by and parked in our driveway. Confirming the call to her before Evan be me up went through; THANK YOU, GOD!!!

Before I could get to the driveway, momma pulled up like a flash of lightning and ran into the house, Nan in toe, me behind her yelling over and over, "I told you not to put your hands on her!" as she beat the brakes off Evan as he shielded his head tucking it in like he was in a tornado drill in elementary school!!!!!!

The police arrived; not sure who called, but as Evan passed by in handcuffs being escorted to the police car after his arrest, looked at me and had the nerve, like a good narcissist, to shift the blame on the scapegoat, stating "you see what you've done?" The dam nerve!

Things calmed down. I left and returned later; Evan wasn't there. The new white kitchen floor my momma took so much pride in still had the black scuff marks from Evan kicking my ass all over the kitchen in his work boots.

Upon his return, I heard him and my momma, who of course never cleared up what took place with me talking. They went into their room and shut the door, and eventually, the lights were out; it wasn't bedtime the girls were still up. I knew what was taking place behind that door, and I was disgusted.

My right shoulder burned from being slid on that floor, and now he was sliding my momma around in the sheets. That was my cue to get the hell out!

After packing I started loading up as much stuff as possible and met up with Cassidy, who stored my television and black art in her mom's trunk. I stayed the night at Shay's. Surprisingly a great idea, his sister and her boyfriend listened to me vent. So much for saving, I was going to have to get into a new lease sooner than expected! One of my "Charlie's Angels admonished me to press charges the following morning. Thankfully court costs were free since I had a police report to prove the assault took place.

# On My Own

I stayed at Shay's for a few nights. I was welcome to stay at Paula's as well. I knew the perfect person to shelter me during the storm that would enjoy some company and an extra couple of dollars, Von!!!! We met in middle school; our birthday was the same day! She was a friend and client for years! She referred many people, and I adored her family, especially her momma Florida.

During high school was over often doing her family's hair. Florida, aka Flo, was a terrific cook. I loved her steak!

Thankfully Von let me move in for a minute. She was expecting a baby and slept most of the time.

# Blessings behind Closed Doors

On the day of court, out of respect for my momma, I went alone, and out of respect for Evan, she went to court with him. I represented myself; Evan was found guilty and, with a dismissed sentence of 2 years, ordered to attend Time Out anger management group for counseling.

Back at momma's house, I was in the kitchen alone after gathering my items, and he just had to say something to me and walked over toward the dining room table where I sat, "if I had gone to jail, you and your momma would be back in the projects!" was his announcement. I just looked at the criminal thinking boy; I got keys to another spot.

The uppity Negro who married a woman from the projects making threats like that needed a good beat down by my Uncle Kenny from the projects! The projects was safer than living in a lovely house with an untrustworthy manipulator. Evan had no idea could bust his balls with my mere words alone.

My exit interview from the house would've put him in cardiac arrest.

Remembering I was not there to visit Evan I marinated in how God had blessed me with my two-bedroom apartment and an excellent job. Wachovia Student Financial Services was sold and purchased by Eduserv Technologies, located off Reynolda Road, five minutes from my new place. Although I was no longer in the W.IS.E. Program, dropped out of Forsyth

Technical Community College, and started going to beauty school at night part-time, I was allowed to keep the job offered to me in Upward Bound through the W.I.S.E. Program full-time.

# Smoke Screens

It felt so good to no longer be under the rule and thumb of momma and Evan! Maya Angelou said it best, "When people show you who they are, believe them!" I "believed" momma put a man before me! I refused to take robotic advice fed to her through Evan while ignoring the ELEPHANT IN THE ROOM any longer!

The first weekend at my new spot, Saturday night Shay was over, pretending he was a visitor.

My furniture was still in storage. I gave him a tour of my two-bedroom and the run-down of my plans to turn the spare room into my salon.

One thing Shay was going to do, if nothing else, was spark up an "L"! I started joking, badgering him, and demanding to know the big deal and why he loved to puff. I decided to try it, and it was so intoxicating I experienced the best sex I had ever had after smoking.

The euphoric moment brought us very close, prolonging his stay, and before you knew it, we were roomies again!

Eventually, the torment and arguments started; his mouth was so disrespectful to stop the noise I locked him out this go-round. No bringing attention to myself yelling!

Christmas Eve had fallen on a Saturday. We were going at it! I took a different approach and escaped him; I left the bedroom and began reading the Bible in the living room, testing the "you can't argue by yourself," theory and he still followed me! The quieter I was, the more he tormented me! I exited the living room and camped out in my walk-in closet, reading scriptures aloud; the boy's mouth was more potent than mine when this didn't help I was pushed to the point of the discovery that my hands worked better than my mouth. Patience would have been a virtue if we were splitting the bills down the middle but the verbal abuse, access to my car, and free room and board made me feel sick at that point of the game!

Bible to the side, out of the closet I started popping my mouth off at him after I resisted as long as I could! The knock at the door came at the perfect time when I tell you God had a way that was mighty sweet! I opened the door and was glad to see my friend/ client Shari and her husband in the form of angels showed up with the Bible cradled in their arms when I had laid my Bible down to fight Shay! Hotdog!!! Who knew what activity they brought to a halt on Christmas Eve?

Shay behaved nicely while they read scriptures and, as time passed, slid to the back respectfully. They offered Christ, and I needed it!

On Christmas Day, I woke up feeling lovely, and I decided to attend Cassidy's church.

Out of Shay's presence, I thought about how reading in my closet to get away from someone in my own house was silly, I'd never do it again!

Shay hopefully would respect my boundaries when I got home we had to talk.

My apartment wasn't a luxury I was in survival mode. Shay had a choice of being home or my place. He would be fine! If his mother was mine, with the excellent care she gave to her three children, there was no telling where I'd be!

"I LOVED HARD," and required that same love in return.

Felt like I had a TSHIRT on with graphics that attracted low vibrational friends, uncaring family members, and lovers void of the ability to give the level of love those that experienced trauma needed.

Being mistreated for so long while treating others the way I wanted to be treated is how I lived my life, the longer I lived it became easy to spot the imbalanced relationships I involve myself in.

# The Reemerge of MIMI

The Crush was doing well for himself, traveling back and forth to different states!

Who knows where we would be if Connor hadn't shown up and pulled the gun on us, luckily he understood I surrendered out of fear when I left him alone in Miss Creekway's living room to go with Connor. I wasn't going to argue with a person that had a gun even if we were broke up!

Thank God Connor's actions didn't overpower the flame we lit in high school to flicker out. Our never-ending friendship was indescribable and fashion was our bond.

Sundays the Crush loved to shop and dine at nice restaurants. I made myself available every time he was in town!

High Point Rd. Greensboro, N.C. was where we escaped shopping! The last stop was dinner. The majority of the time we dined at our favorite restaurant, Grady's Grill. The apple pie alamode was a must have and I wasn't even that big on dessert.

A summer day out with a handsome guy exposing me to the finer things of life was a pleasure! Laughter and the best music filled the car during the thirty-minute drive there and back.

Not many guys would treat me in the manner The Crush did, without strings attached.

When I met Mia at fifteen I stated I wanted a man to take care of me like guys made sure she was straight. The opportunity presented itself to get things I needed when he popped the trunk of his Sterling loaded with money, but something down on the inside of me simply was appreciative of our time together and the money he spent on my shopping.

Mia definitely would've asked for some cash, after seeing all those loose bills.

The Crush expressed in our teens that I liked clowns. The statement upset me initially, but he may have been correct.

Love wouldn't be enough in my future relationships. In high school, romance and chocolate candy were fine, but after graduation the way my bills were set up and as hard as I worked, whoever I dated next would have to work just as hard!

# Uncle Miles

The thing I loved most about being on my own was the ability to come and go anywhere I wanted and no adult could stop me! One of my favorite places to go was to see Uncle Miles and Aunt Polly. I loved momma sisters and they treated me like a niece and I felt so at home at their house!

Uncle Miles, Coolie's younger Brother was 15 years older than me and I loved him DEARLY!!! He was the baby boy of the family and he put in the most effort to show me he was there for me and made me feel like a niece! Every time I saw him he gave me a $10 bill. Many things made Uncle Miles stand out differently than his siblings. His love was disconnected from religion he absolutely genuinely cared about people regardless of their religious beliefs. Uncle Miles move to the beat of his own drum and he would kick your ass if he needed to. He parked out front where Coolie parked. He washed his car out front and every one of his friends around that car hanging out cutting up with him knew I was his niece when they saw me and he interacted with me. These things are customary for humans but were very important out to me because many of my relatives were not involved the way I plan to be involved with my nieces and nephews and grandchildren on the future.

# Coming of Age

It was my birthday weekend, and I was single! Shay's sister Vet and I got close when after she and Shay became roommates, and we had plans to see Biggie Smalls.

21 was a milestone. I wanted to celebrate myself!

Unsure of what I wanted to wear, I headed to the mall in search of something that screamed MICHELLE is older!

Denim was my favorite material to wear. Walking past The Limited, an ankle-length -sleeveless denim shirt dress with silver hardware and side splits caught my eye. The $80 tag made me hope the dress was on sale! I should've been on the clearance rack, but not for my birthday, so I splurged a little!!! Aldo had the perfect boots. My look was complete!

Cassidy was pregnant, so I decided to ride with Vet so she could drive my car and parking lot pimp. We loved to be on the scene; outside, the club would be just as busy as the inside! People were coming in droves for the show. The car was in great hands I taught her how to operate a straight drive; I knew she'd be fine. Besides, I'd want someone to do that for me.

Vet and I road by Neal's to grab tickets before the concert; Cassidy was out and about but Darius was driving! I walked up to the vehicle, and they immediately got out at the stoplight! Cassidy was pregnant; I wasn't going to upset her like him driving my car angered me. Upon my approach when I saw the doors open I assumed he and Cassidy were switching seats, but he walked off, and she followed. I watched the back of their heads get small. Momma and Evan taught me well I wasn't a match for pillow talk, so I knew not to run after them. Women put men before their children; friendship wasn't any different; that night her man came first.

Sheesh, I was in the car with someone else, trying to enjoy myself! Cassidy could've jumped in the driver's seat and driven off in the moonlight and I could've continued my night; I blamed myself!

Pissed, I jumped into the driver's side and moved the car.

Cassidy and I never discussed where they walked off to or how she got home. I never told her how leaving my car at the intersection was disrespectful because I'm the fool for treating her like I wanted to be treated!

# Amusement Parks

Brielle and Von were mutual friends of Cassidy and I from Kennedy Middle School. During an appointment, they jokingly chanted, "you put that girl out of that car!" followed by bursts of laughter like hyenas! Amused, I entertained them with the truth as I did their hair. Sadly, I was naive. The young ladies I "thought" were my friends got a kick out of bringing up this lie. I didn't understand what was funny about not knowing where my friend went, but I knew "Confusion comes from the enemy." Only a frenemy got joy out of others' pain.

I "met" and meshed with Brielle and Von in middle school but "selected" Cassidy as a friend literally via a handwritten letter. The friendship Cassidy and I had "was" without spot wrinkles or blemishes "before that messiness!"

Things got awkward. It took me a minute to recover; I no longer felt as relaxed in the friendship. No one is perfect but talking about my best friend to some chicks we knew gossiped wasn't "my character"!

The report "I put a pregnant girl out of the car" was rolling around like a wheelbarrow! Of course, no discussion of why he was driving my damn car without permission arose!!!!!

They had no idea I had 99 problems at my momma's house and I was providing a service to survive.

My Defense mechanisms were on high alert! I knew if I reacted, we would no longer be friends. I cannot explain why I cared.

How they knew the situation even took place ate me up the most! Triggering reminders of my dynamic with Evan saying things concerning me to the others that like one sided stories. Maybe there wasn't enough brain storage to sync both sides of the story.

Any spirit that enjoyably OVERPOWERED my truth was low-key trying to hurt me.

I hadn't arrived, but I prided myself on my wholesomeness and good reputation as a future stylist. Why hell would I put a pregnant woman out of the car???

The church, Upward Bound, interactions with adults at the bank, shampooing at "Hair by Alexander" and chopping it up with grown-ass ladies who patronized me to get their hair done gave me a mature edge. My heart was involved so although red flags were there I continued in the friendship.

# Living Single

Being single was liberating after a lengthy relationship since 8th grade. Sundays were very peaceful; I enjoyed church and visiting family.

Natalie was the only client that scheduled on Sundays, she liked to return to Charlotte for school at J.C.S.U. with freshly done hair; she was very fly, go figure! Evenings after I finished visiting family she and her Cool ass Jamaican boyfriend that treated her like a queen would arrive!

Natalie and I attended middle school together, but our paths never crossed; Von referred her and was our mutual friend. A season arrived; we became friends after having dynamic conversations with her and her man. I grew to respect her because, like myself, we were both from the projects aspiring to become something GREAT in life despite our roots! Unfortunately, the love of her life, Donte, was killed! Natalie eventually moved back to Winston-Salem, and we started hanging out.

The Club "Baby Shamus" Paula and Mia went to on Wednesday after I did their hair when I was a high schooler was still open and jumping! Finally, I was 21, old enough to go! Word on the street, if you arrived before ten, entry was FREE!!! This idea was genius. More money for drinks!!!

The mall closed at nine, and after grabbing something to wear, I conveniently arrived before 10; it would be so empty, leaving unnoticed was not easy! Midnight-ish, after I showered and dressed, I returned to crowded streets and a full-blown party inside!

Thursdays, my first stop was "On the Fringe" for Karaoke Night. The food was good, and the drinks were always plentiful! Encounters with old acquaintances and past male interests resurfaced, glad to purchase my alcoholic beverages. It seemed like I had been under a rock seeing all the faces from high school. On The Fringe was the meetup spot before going to Neals' Night Club. I ran into my "GOOD JUDY," Talena, knowing she was back in NC from Tennessee, made my night!

We exchanged numbers; the timing was perfect. She, Natalie, and I started hanging out in Greensboro at club Side Effects getting our drink on!

221

# Sensations of Side Effects

Greensboro is where Al B. swept me off my feet and bought us drinks; he was a little older than me; his curly hair and chocolate skin made me blush! I was so captivated by him I stayed overnight in Greensboro with him after we left the club.

New York guys were different, I noticed!

Al was a North Carolina A&T graduate and a Q-Dog like my dad. Like a gentleman, he drove when we went out, and he paid every time. I love foosball, and funny on our first date at this Pub in Greensboro, there stood a foosball table when we entered. I took it easy on him as we played after placing our order.

My hamburger and baked beans taste so good I didn't care that I smashed my plate in the presence of a guy I liked!

# Up Norf Trip

Peace sent a Western Union transfer for me to purchase my train ticket to New York!

Life was sweet! I had gotten used to being in my place alone. Being single seemed like a disease to some, but not to me; I was thoroughly enjoying myself!

The night before traveling to N.Y., I ran into Trista at D' Elegance. Thursday nights were more relaxed than Wednesdays, so we chatted and created huge haze clouds, and sipped. I got her phone number with plans to reach out when I return.

It was my first time in New York City, "The Big City of Dreams!" Feeling pretty and stoked, I was a little nervous traveling so far alone. Peace pulled up to get me in a Town Car that Friday evening from Grand Central Station, and every regret left.

Dinner was our first stop. Peace egged me on to try Sake' a Japanese liquor concocted from fermented rice. I was expecting a shot glass when the waitress presented me with a dainty three-piece white tea set; a cup on the saucer, from the flute, emerged clear hot liquor. Pinky extended bottoms up, smoothly it went down and warmness coated my insides. Momma "charm school" taught ladies to order mixed drinks and always watch their glasses coinciding with Charles Angel's warnings about people slipping you "A Mickey." I couldn't keep my eyes off the flute consisting of two refills awaiting me!!

Dinner was AWESOME. I loosened up as I took in the lights and action of the city that never sleeps!! I highly recommend women including momma try shots of Sake'!

My hotel was on Long Island, where I surprisingly ran into Eric Sermon.

I was suspicious when Peace didn't stay all night; it was fine with me.

Friday night was so live Saturday morning that I slept late. After speaking with him and his friends back home, I was excited to explore my surroundings alone. Long Island was beautiful; the shopping centers and landscaping reminded me of North Carolina.

Peace arrived at about 1 p.m. at the hotel Saturday with a driver, a plan, and some smoke to pull on as the young driver headed towards the city.

Jamaica Ave. in Queens N.Y. flea market "The Coliseum," blew my mind; it had to be the biggest Flea Market I had ever visited! Beepers were in all styles and flavors! Reasonably priced lingerie and undergarments! Stuff for sale was everywhere!

Next, we headed to Midtown, Manhattan to site see. The elevator ride to the top of the Empire State Building was epic! I looked over the city with binoculars.

Saturday night, we saw a movie in a 12 cinema theater which was unheard of in N.C., and to dinner.

Peace was the perfect gentleman all weekend. Like the Crush, he didn't pressure me about sex; we just had fun! All I could think of was what we would do when he and his people came to North Carolina Memorial Day Weekend!

# Brown Girl Joy Reunion

I caught up with Trista when I returned, and we clubbed so foolishly, we decided it would be financially feasible to become roommates.

So many perks came with her presence! We both were molded as homemakers growing up with lots of responsibility around the house! Cooking was her expertise! I hadn't mastered it as well.

Thanks to Trista's driver's license I could escape from our boring side of town to the Northside. I never dreamed together we'd have had a north-side address!

The apartment was stocked full of food, smoke, and Trista's Henny, which became my favorite drink and had a nice feel to it!

Weekends after my clients, Sade or Mobb Deep blasted through the apartment as we got ready to go out for the night.

Every day was fun! I welcomed her presence before she moved in because she has always offered Zen!

# Madam Tours

Butterflies fluttered my tummy the whole month of May!

Memorial Day weekend! Peace's visit went down in history! He and his friends enjoyed NC!

My friends assisted me in showing them a great time. I prided myself on the southern tour I gave them. Greensboro Nightlife delighted them!! Peace blasted N.Y. mixed tapes that attracted female club goers to his Black Lincoln Continental with New York plates blasting DJ Clue.

Peace visits to North Carolina became frequent! Bookie, his best friend was more so "my type," and was always throwing jabs and provoking me! Laying on the couch something heavy plopped on me as they entered unannounced; it was Bookie's beautiful yellow pet snake, Penelope, I would've slapped him if it was a dog or cat!!! Unbelievably this was my introduction to his snake.

The strides they made during their move to North Carolina were impressive! Their entourage had a hungry breed of males. Wealth was their focus more so than pleasure. Chatting on the phone with Peace, I overheard his sister flip on him in the background because panties that belonged to "someone" was mixed in with the laundry she did for him. From the sounds of it, that wasn't a part of the deal to do his laundry.

# New Neighbors

The new neighbors moved in; I was thrilled to find out it was Sunny and Victoria from the Girl's Club and RJR! Connor and the girls were thick as thieves growing up; they were as cool as he had described!

The sisters effortlessly carved beautiful ocean and scrunch waves that turned everybody's head! They had the city on lockdown.

It was nothing for us to borrow hair supplies and stuff from each other! Who would've ever thunk we would evolve into such a way after knowing them for years!!

# Linked IN

Visits with Cassidy were always full of life and excitement!

Cassidy pregnancy was moving along fast. July 18 was getting closer!

The girl's love for vegetables enhanced carrying the baby. Cassidy ate vegetables and no meat before being vegan was hip!!

My freezer door swung off the hinge during her ice-craving stage, if I allowed she would've eaten all my ice!

Super mounds of voluminous curls billowed around her face. Like a good sister-friend, one day sitting around the apartment as "I'm Cool Like That" played, and I decided to shape her hair, similar to the curly afro the rapper Butterfly donned! In my eyes, they favored. Cassidy looked crazy fly in her natural essence, the pregnancy gave her a glow.

Despite the damper the car situation caused, Cassidy brought me joy and both of us could find laughter in anything we did! God was our common denominator! Many had no idea as they observed us dance to rap music that we sang gospel songs when said the Lord!

Ebony and Ivory vibes are what we gave off every meetup!

# Unladylike

Sundays in the spring and summer, I loved going to church regardless of what time Trista and I crawled in from the streets.

Keeping the Sunday tradition was a big deal in my family. It made Nan so happy to see me in my Sunday best, just like when I was a child, but this Sunday I preferred laying around to relish in the most eventful time of my young life!

God knows the life I craved to live as a young girl, and slowly it was manifesting!

Natalie loved Jamaicans, and after last night I know why! What a sweet hangover I had the morning after a night with Mike, my new Jamaican beau; he was all I could think about; the church wasn't on my mind this Sunday!

I loved everything that took place; the emphasis Mike put on Mi.' when he said Michelle in his Jamaican accent drove me crazy!

God knows I had a thing for guys from New York Mike's Caribbean roots were a bonus.

We bumped into each other at the bar in The Nightclub, Neals. The dark, handsome chocolate statue seemed powerful. One drink and conversation turned into drinks for all my friends! We danced and grinned and sipped all night with him and his guys! The song selection "You Make Me Feel (Like a Natural Woman)," is what came to mind, I felt super sexy around him as he quickly swept me off my feet.

Hanging out with a man after 2 am you met at the club was unladylike, but the way he grabbed my hands and led me towards the exit with "all eyes on me" like we had just celebrated our 1st anniversary that night felt good. The spirit of nosey sprinkled with judgment was a characteristic I knew all too well. After the break up with Connor, I strictly portrayed "single and loving it!" up until tonight, any romantic moves I made were privatized. Thrilled at what the night entailed; I was all in!

The classy exit to the car out front was so New York! Mike revealed a fresh unopened bottle of Courvoisier before the driver pulled off and gave "let's keep the party going" sparks in my brain. I was intoxicated, but aware provisions had been made so no one risked their life driving drunk before pulling off with our friends in tow. The destination we arrived at was a hotel off Stratford Rd.

Once everyone was inside the pretty foyer mingling took place. Making it my business to be uncountrified, not one immature bone stood out in my 21- year-old body as I worked the room, only speaking when spoken to, and replying with answers from the mind of a Paula and Mia.

Unsure if it was Mike or the liquor but I could've got used to nights like this!  Where the hell all these handsome New Yorkers had been hiding, I thought to myself as we rubbed elbows with them and other classy natives of the city.

The penthouse suite upstairs with conjoined rooms for his friends and the carloads of girls was the final destination.

New Yorkers God connected me with were goal-oriented. Conversations were about future business openings and making money.

Funny people were judged for clubbing because class was in session when I was around them; the spirit of "get money" jumped on me.

My brain was very stimulated by that nucleus of men on a Sunday morning before the church doors opened at 11 a.m.! The church should've taught what I learned from them that night. The older I got, I realize indoctrination took place in churches. Come Sunday, Pastor taught lessons I learned as a kid in Sunday school; it was never about the member's financial expansion. The church labeled these men I was in the company of as "worldly," ignoring they're common denominator to expand financially. The unbreakable bonds between them and the loyalty they displayed were something I rarely witnessed at church.

The morning "Social" was moving into 4 am. Mike was a gentleman, and I felt safe in his arms and tipsy too, but I wasn't spending the night.

The intelligent conversation we had made Mike even more attractive. Settling down for a man like him became a consideration. I had one minor scare when Tariq, who rode in the car with us, entered the room unannounced. The only thing open that late was legs! My heart rate went up, hoping I hadn't given an impression they both could have me. Thank God, he just had a question. I was glad he burst in; it was the perfect time to end a beautiful night. It felt good to peel the covers away in front of Tariq, fully clothed. Nan didn't raise a fool!

# Boys to Men

Entry to both of the clubs in the city I frequented was now free and included a tab for drinks thanks to Mike! Saturday after doing hair I had awesome anticipation about the thrilling night to come! After the club, we went to his condo and my place once. Every moment with him was EUPHORIC! Mike could not reach me sometimes because I didn't keep the battery in my pager fresh, so he gave me $50 to buy batteries!

Male peers I grew up with no longer caught my attention; the town was small, and I was private! Dating someone everybody knew got old. Connor, The Crush, and Shay are great guys, but Al, Peace, and Mike were more refreshing.

D Elegance on Wednesday was a constant. Mike mainly patronized Neal's, so I didn't see him until Thursday.

The TREFO was full of whispers about a Land Cruiser with New York plates that read "Big Willy" zooming around the city. I got a glimpse of it and the driver's profile in passing one afternoon on the way to Nan's. Where I'm from, driving around in vehicles without the income to back it up brought unwanted attention to one's self. The NY plates made matters worse. The town was talking about him like a celebrity flew in. Unfortunately, an illness that caused people to get sick or nauseous when they see someone blessed ran rampant in Winston called "hate." The haters brought attention to you that possibly got you robbed; then there was the hater with criminal cases that informed WSPD and the District Attorney to get less or no time.

Well, well, well, it was "T," aka Big Willy, in the flesh, at D Elegance, aka Baby Shamus. He was easy on the eyes, but that cop magnet he drove gave me "locked up" vibes, so I paid him no mind as he attempted to kick it with me with cocky and arrogant mannerisms. The handsome chocolate guy rooting for him to get my number caught my attention when he entered the building before I made the connection that the two of them arrived together. The tall, lean young man captivated my soul when he sat at the table with a big smile explaining "his man" liked me in his NY accent. I answered in two words, "I'm good!" Hilariously I cracked up knowing my "clown phase" was over. I'm sure the hearts in momma's eyes when she was around Evan had taken over my pupils because as crazy as I seemed while chatting it up with him on the inside my heart I held an indescribable love for the stranger sitting across from me and it was void of sexual thoughts. I did not go there for that purpose; it was beyond me. Mike was more of an infatuation; I didn't feel love. Sober, I could've sat and listened to him talk without knowing his name for eternity, I thought to myself as I turned back to continue conversing with the LOVE OF MY LIFE, who was poof, gone, and nowhere to be found after turning my back briefly to saying hello to someone that spoke to me.

I slept, hoping to see him in my dreams; he never showed up.

# Reminisce

Neal's was hosting a concert "after party." Oddly I was asked to pay to enter when I bypassed the window. At the bar, the drinks weren't freely accessible anymore, so I paged Mike after paying to enter like the "good ole days!"

A lump was in my throat; my body temperature felt warm and stuffy. Mike walks in with this lady! My eyes must have dilated in disbelief and embarrassment! Mike conversed with his daughter's mother, Shelby, on the phone, in front of me, but debuting her that night let me know she was more than a "baby momma"!! The idiot had the nerve to introduce us as I approached to confront him. I wanted to know why Shelby was there!

My friends pulled me out of the club, crying! It wasn't the night I imagined! Feeling stupid, I got home early that night.

# Whew CHIIIIIIILD

$M$y adolescent eyes saw clearly that my family dynamic was different than others. I often talked to God and asked what I did to deserve the family he sent me to. Both of my parents had new families and did a terrific job parenting the kids of those they married just fine, but they didn't seem to have operating instructions for Michelle.

Regardless I took the initiative to gain a relationship with Coolie. He was battling his own demons but his dating life was developing noticeably fine as he exposed a beautiful woman in photos from a beach trip they took.

Coolie was clueless; I had never been to the beach and didn't care to ask if I had ever been.

Soon they were married.

Omitted from the guest list, of course, Coolie showed me the dam pictures!!!

Tormented, REJECTION BLANKET on hurt, I took in how grand the event was. He had married well.

Not inviting me to the wedding was no different than no invite to dinner, The same people that told family "you know you don't need no invitation" when you missed dinner were invited; aware of the date and time and walked past my house on the way to their car.

I couldn't walk to their wedding.

Coolie and mom didn't co-parent before he met his first wife Valencia, nor did he include me in their family circle after their union.

# Big Sis

I prayed for God to send me siblings. My brother Yancy arrived the same year as Emily; I wasn't introduced to him. Encounters between us still only occurred when I crept up to grandmas at the sight of Coolie's car when I visited Nan. My brother possessed beautiful green eyes that spoke to you even when he was silent.

I saw Emily fresh out of the womb! Nan and I watched the nurse clean the afterbirth off of her. I was even blessed to witness her first hair shampoo done with a long brush that looked like you could clean the bathtub, used to scrub her hair. Brooklyn's birth, I wasn't present, but we bonded once she arrived home. I greeted her with a lovely scalp massage. Years later, in gym class, Coach Watkins, my dad's friend, congratulated me on the new addition to the family. The news was exciting, although hearing my sister was born from Coolie would've been better.

The entire school year, Coach Watkins made me aware every the time he saw my dad, I wanted to lean towards his ear like I was going to whisper and then yell; I HAVEN'T EVEN TALKED TO THAT MAN!!!

My experience with the siblings Coolie created was nonexistent. If I weren't significant enough for "him" to contact on their day of birth, I wouldn't be of importance to them. Living in separate households from Yancy and Yasmine should not have interfered with our bond. These grown tail adults with cars living less than 6 minutes apart from one another made sure they bonded with "their" siblings but didn't provide us with the same opportunities as their children!!!!!

# Omega Sigh

Q Dogs be like, "You may have another sister," I wasn't shocked as I examined the photo of a pretty little brown girl named Bella who looked to be age 5 or 6. I commended him for sharing because I was polite, but I had no idea what he wanted me to do or say. SMH, He sat on this information and had slept on a relationship with me for years.

Visits I initiated with the desire to connect with my brother and sister, Yancy and Yasmine didn't take place until I could drive. Now I'd have a 4th sister to cultivate a relationship with way from Rocky Mount. Until that day, I hadn't heard mention of the city my new sister was born and raised.

My dad and his home girl arranged for the family to receive Bella at

Grandma Maury's, and just like that, I loved her as if we hadn't missed 16 years of each other's life.

My little sister was beautiful, tall, and had a runner's body! She ran track and carried herself very maturely. We both were at an age we could relate, especially to being stepchildren!!! Bella and I were intentional about connecting. I enjoyed our long conversations.

We both hunted Coolie and initiated relationships with him. She desired to send him that photo I saw and meet him. Bella requested her mother's friend Gail set up the meeting; I called her the angelic liaison to Coolie over the years.

Bella and I controlled the development of our sisterhood.

We were the determiners of our future, with or without Coolie. "I" loved him regardless of the hurt from his rejection, we both shared.

My attempts to connect with Coolie were daughterly, his inability to connect with me on a fatherly level hurt. I was in the habit of being around people that hurt me because I grew up in a home with people who hurt me.

# I Got Company

I invited Bella to visit during her spring break. She drove the 2 1/2 hour drive; by the way, her boyfriend accompanied her. I was speechless, her momma who btw was a Leo-like momma, and Valencia; permitted a boy to tag along!

We ate out, went to the mall, and stayed up late! I was determined to do sisterly things with Bella during her visit. The long conversations in person were priceless.

Yancy and Yasmine had never spent the night with me, I was amazed how that one visit brought Bella and me so close. Living in the same city I imagined how enriched the bonds between my brother and sister could've been with multiple visits similar to that one visit Bella and I were blessed to have.

# I Knew When I Laid Eyes on Him

Trista got off work at three. I was off from work that humid Monday afternoon and surprised her outside when she got off. BDP, aka Boston Housing Projects, was right around the corner, so we headed to Oak Street. Sunny and Victoria moms' porch was running over. I pulled over immediately! Trista's guy friend's family yard was full of folks too.

I walked up, and to my surprise, there sat THE LOVE of my LIFE, Big Willy's friend that disappeared in thin air from the club!!!

So many paid, handsome fellas that I knew were present. I kept calm despite his presence moving on after I acknowledged the New Yorker, then headed inside to say hello to Mrs. San, the lady of the house.

Fire from Jamaica and his Jamaican friends were rolling up with bible pages on my way inside, which was both exciting and cringy. This Monday felt like Friday.

Thankfully the stranger hadn't vanished; he was still on the porch, and I couldn't wait to see what was up! Finally, I had a name to go with that face! "Cliff," and I chopped it up a while. He was three years older than me, with soft, curly hair I had to control my hands from touching.

I gave him my number. He didn't call that night or week, which puzzled me. I eventually forgot he had my number.

Weeks later, on a Saturday afternoon, I finished working early, the phone rang, and it was him calling!!!!!!!

During our conversation, I invited him over after he asked what I was doing. Excitement and butterflies fluttered in my stomach for the first time in a long time!

Cliff arrived just as Trista, her cousin Midge and Kenzie were leaving. He acted like he was roasting as he walked in and took his shirt off! Embarrassed, I introduced everyone to him shirtless. He "was" sweating. I was blushing; a lot commenced when he arrived that wasn't permissible in the "south," especially the first visit to someone's house. The guy needed pointers from Nan's Charm

School.

My Southern morals were eating at me as I tried to be a gracious host in my short shorts and fav mid-drift million-dollar babe graphic T- shirt, no bra, just like in Atlanta.

A date typically took place first, but with no regrets, I let go and went with the flow. I peeked out while slightly closing the blinds and all the cars looked familiar, so I didn't even know how Cliff had arrived but was under the impression he could buy a car if he wanted to. The guy was getting away with a lot in the first five minutes in the door.

I closed the blinds for privacy and the stigma left on me after living with a "Peeping Tom." Cliff made himself very comfortable and exuded confidence. I hope the change in the lighting didn't send off the wrong signal.

We puffed and watched music videos. Males came by to puff with Trista and me all the time, interested in us; it usually was no big deal. Cliff affected me differently than those encounters. I forget I ever dated anyone else in the presence of what seemed like a familiar stranger. Maybe his bare chest was affecting me. The proper church girl Nan raised extended the invite to him during the day to avoid confusion as if sex didn't occur in broad daylight. Euphoria in the air made me trash my morals. 21-year-old Michelle wasn't the Michelle Nan raised; I exuded sexiness that I never asked for that attached to me growing up in a house of lust and porn seasoned with experiences with Connor.

That afternoon entertaining Cliff; the Lady that came alive in me pondered what to call a one-night stand when it happened during the day.

Without shame in my decision I made to give into the passion between Cliff and me; surprisingly thoughts of being "a whore," didn't haunt me, although whores entertained strangers.

After our time together that day, he wasn't just a homeboy stopping by.

Cliff walked around nude, causing me to reflect on how quick I was to cover up my body I gained an appreciation for that day after he encouraged me that my "grown lady body was going to be nice," very Gynecologist like; whatever that meant, I looked forward to it! Regardless of how many people told me how sexy I was, I hated the attention and felt underweight. His pep talk boosted my ego.

Covering up and dressing in the dark growing up, I could appreciate Cliff's chiseled body and joined his nudist colony!

Starving, he suggested dinner. I wanted Cassidy to meet him. Cliff treated us to Quincy's Steakhouse, and I dropped him off at the bus station. We laughed and talked till his bus arrived. A sadness overcame me as I watched the bus pull onto the highway. From that day forward, we kept in close touch permanently! I had been bitten by the love bug.

Peace and his boys were back in North Carolina. I liked him. I'm sure he was waiting for the day to come for intimacy but linking up with Cliff changed things. He still came by. Luckily he and Cliff never came by at the same time. Peace eventually started chilling with my neighbors. We remained friends.

# Summer of 95

I ran the streets and wound down in the evenings with Cliff. If I wasn't at home, I stayed in Cliff's hotel room. A friend accompanied me and hung out in the bed right across from us with one of his friends.

I preferred my place because checkout time came quickly; we talked and laughed till the wee hours of the morning.

This summer was the best. On my most memorable night, the breeze cooled off our naked bodies under my bedroom window as we gazed at the stars. Cliff told me of the many dreams he wanted for his family. Listening intently, I examined my life.

My care for money lessened. The gas tank stayed full, and we ate out frequently. I liked that Cliff always asked if I needed anything.

The guy was easygoing and loved watching sports and going to the movies! I would secretly cry when he left town and look forward to his calls until he returned.

I thought I was in the know when he touched down. A collect call from the local jail changed that. Without questioning him as a southern girl should before involving herself, he gave me the number of a lawyer to reach out to, explained that someone was stopping by, and gave instructions. The knock at the door came not too long after the call. "A FEMALE," a young lady named

Jenifer I knew of but not personally had arrived, I'm guessing on his behalf. I'm sure she had the same questions I had swarming in her head if he had made her feel like I felt around him. She gave me money and a large container and left. I hit the blinds to see what kind of car she was in for future ref. I got a little nauseous. I loved my new $20,000 Periwinkle Blue Toyota Paseo until I saw her Coupe with leather seats. My ass went to test drive a Charcoal Grey Jetta like Mia's for 10,000 less and left in a Toyota.

Next, I needed to see what was inside the large container. It was Cliff's neatly folded clothing; he had great taste. I was also now in possession of a nice amount of cash! I could be trusted and was willing to help, no questions asked.

I met the lawyer with the bail money and soon after received a call that I could pick him up. He was grinning when he walked out. His smile was grand with his gorgeous teeth. Nothing could shake his spirit, and neither would I with questions about his profession! Of course, we went to eat and then home, glued to each other.

# Lay Your Head on my Pillow

Home is where the heart is. Cuffing season was coming upon us early. Cliff and I woke up together from that day forward. Trista was cozied up with Flippa. We all meshed well.

Cassidy had the baby; she was back on the scene and at the house hanging out, mixing well with his friends. I had a feeling fall 1995 would be like no other!

Cliff was his own man, when it came to handling his business, I wasn't his only go-to. Via phone call, a constituent from Cleveland Projects made me aware while I worked, and Jenifer and Cliff came through. The man made me feel hot and bothered, she may have been effected in that same manner! Casting down every vain imagination of thoughts of them sleeping together that crept into my head was not easy! Clarity if Cliff was a user or on some pimp shit; living with me, getting rides from her would come.

Nan called New Yorkers city slickers. This was some city-slicker 256 shit!

If the spark between them still sparkled, and I don't mean from a lighter, he could go on and live his life!

Running at the first mishap in my relationships may have caused me to miss blessings. I believe we met on purpose and decided not to disengage.

Transmission of AIDS among other things surrounded by the possibility of sharing lovers caused resistance to questioning Cliff to flee. Despite the woman dropping off all his clothes and bail money to my crib; according to him, Jenifer was "KD's friend." Unaware I had the rundown on the car seating chart; I let him jabber on, knowing KD sat in the backseat, and sometimes they rode solo. Matching his energy, I stopped going straight home from work like a submissive dummy and remembered the single woman I was, and made a pit stop over at Shay's to exhale in a cloud.

Shay was moving on with his life; I noticed, looking through a shoe box of his bike rally pictures, shocked to come across my sweet grinning, head-covered Muslim friend Sasha from Upward Bound nude! Dam, she fooled me, or maybe I was naive. Shay was too embarrassed, we laughed like brothers and sisters as we puffed.

In the meantime, word on the streets Mike got busted and broke his legs jumping out the window and trying to evade the cops. I wouldn't say I liked that for him, but I got over it when I remembered the scene at Neal's the last time I saw him. God had other plans for my life.

# Movers and Shakers

Teeka was doing big things after premiering in Essence Magazine, and she made plans to move to the A. I graciously took over her lease per her request! It was an upgrade for me and a power move for her! I was ecstatic; my friend from the 1st grade was making a name for herself. I admired her for leaving all her clients behind to model.

Peace and Bookie popped up over at my crib. Cliff was out of town, thank God they just walked in, and I felt something heavy fall on me; Bookie brought his snake to North Carolina!! It had white and yellow skin and was huge! I wasn't scared of snakes but terrified of dogs and cats! Bookie was easy on the eyes and more my type, to be honest.

We did not get along. He always provoked me with a smile on his face proclaiming, "I'm just playing."

These two were serious about moving to North Carolina. Hating to miss them when I moved, I gave them the news; they asked me to move in.

Cliff wanted the place also when I shared it with him. I knew mixing business, and pleasure was wrong, but I naturally told Cliff yes; I felt he would be a part of my future.

# Positive and Negatives

$E$arly fall, I settled into the apartment, which was literally on the same street, one minute away from my old place! Trista and I hadn't been living there long. Cliff was at my spot mainly, and his friends chilled at the old apartment when they were in town.

Still 21, single, and ready to mingle.

I woke up and, out of habit, lit a cigarette like any other morning, but I couldn't smoke. Something wasn't right. I wasn't trying to quit; whatever was going on with my body delivered me from smoking!

Trista gladly took the cigarettes off my hand after I handed her the pack!

I scheduled a doctor's appointment for October 16. No insurance; the same Planned Parenthood I had visited with a coworker for moral support is where I decided to go. Just like her, I was pregnant, five weeks!

The birthing process and visual length of the epidural needle haunted me. I vowed to have no kids, but without a doubt, I was adamant I was keeping my baby! Feelings of joy and nervousness came as I drove! Pride said you don't even know this guy; he's from over 500 miles away! The world wanted to swallow me whole, my bills couldn't be to me, regardless of my financial status!

I was mute and had no input when I got pregnant by Shay. Momma should've involved everyone, EVEN ME, before making such a COLOSSAL decision. Shay's family loved children! Momma set up an abortion and I never knew why she had her teen baby and got rid of mine.

I tried hard not to be like momma, but I would've graduated pregnant just like her

Many of the European girls were there from other cities which were pretty crafty.

You couldn't eat anything before the "procedure." Nurses offered oatmeal cakes and Pepsi afterward; they admonished us to eat to replenish sugar levels from blood loss. I'll never forget it. We went across the street to the mall. I ate Chic Fila.

Mrs. Creekway wanted all the details when I called her. My room was dark; the television was on; I was in a trance as I spoke, unconscious of what I had participated in that day. It made me wonder if my existence was centered on a lack of money and if this was how she and Coolie avoided the same route in the 70s she had me take in the 90s.

Momma's was the first place I went. I was so happy!!! She called everybody in the kitchen after I gave her the news; before I could get it out, she blurted out, "Chelle, pregnant!" My sisters started yelling and jumping!

Even though momma loved her husband and family more than I,

I went there first because it's natural to share news of your pregnancy with your parents, in my case, momma. Coolie and I were distant. Eventually, Grandma Maury would tell him. I did her and Aunt Mary's hair every other Saturday morning.

Afterward, I headed to my old apartment; Cliff and his friends were glued to the TV, watching The Million Man March. It was quiet, and so was I when I walked in and focused on Farrakhan's speech with the men. When the opportunity presented itself, I told Cliff I had something to talk to him about outside. It was a fantastic day to give him the news; the speech on The Black Family to the men made me lose my nervous edge.

Cliff was happy with the news, revealing a mature side; he began to speak about the responsibility of having a child; he said things to me like a father warning his daughter. The talk made me feel like a child wanting shoes that don't fit. I wasn't ready, but I was willing to get as prepared as I could!

That night Cliff stayed at his place. Rejection and I went back to my place. It had been a minute since I had been alone. Sad is what I chose to be apart from him because I wasn't mature enough to respect that maybe Cliff needed space to digest the information.

Quietly in bed, I lay with my thoughts. The timeline was so short; church girl with an unborn child conceived in two months of knowing the father would embarrass many!

The following morning I was headed out. Cliff was coming back from the store for coffee and the newspaper; he jumped in the car we talked some more. Every conversation we had was priceless; as crazy as it sounded, this was my child's father I was conversing with about a child I never knew we would create!

The pregnancy allowed me a glimpse into Cliff's life. He was an uncle to two nieces; his sister's daughter hung out with him during the day while his sister worked. I loved knowing this about him. It took a village to raise a child!

Plans changed; I did not renew the lease at the old place. Cliff and I would enjoy the new space. Trista and I monumental season came to a close, as fun as it was.

Cliff I met at the club was more fun than Pre-fatherhood Cliff. This discovery taught me not to judge a book by its cover. Boys supposedly matured slower than girls, but our maturity levels were different. He was waaaayyy more mature than I was. Cliff began to prepare to be a father. I did nothing other than quit smoking, pray and love him. We had qualities that benefitted both of us. "Cash rules everything around me" was just a song I danced to before we met but became a paper-chasing affirmation.

I was 21 for six months, learning a lifetime of lessons from a man

I barely knew that Coolie should've taught me.

My complaints about my life seemed shallow, observing how Cliff tackled life without his parents. Cliff came from the loins of a father nicknamed "Stacks" and the womb of a mother known not to "F" within, their community. My esteem was low coming from the loins of Coolie, a nonparticipant in my life and a momma blinded in love. I hated to make comparisons but it was all I had to make sense of my life.

# Playing House

For once, I was not struggling. Cliff cared for me as no man ever had. I handled this relationship with "kid gloves" because he earned my respect. I didn't badger him, I gave him breathing room.

While he traveled, I upgraded the bedroom's look. My taste was changing. I invested in a luxurious Burlington House bedspread and sheer curtains. The cream and gold tapestry print made me feel royal, and it screamed parents! On the weekends, I spent time with friends going to dinner, and the movies were also enjoyable on weekends.

"Count on me" was played in the cinema when Natalie and I went to see "Waiting to Exhale," the song touched me so profoundly that I purchased the soundtrack. Every morning I played and sang the song to my stomach repeatedly on the way to work.

My daily routine changed. Morning sickness allotted me unexpected days off. I was an early riser and raised to let the man of the house sleep; with no desire for television, I walked into the second bedroom to examine it and visualize it with baby decor and drifted over to the window, absorbing in my newsfeed at the most peaceful time of the day. Scanning the room, I walked over to the empty closet and imagined it was full of baby clothes, and began to talk to God about making a way to purchase the clothes; my only source had been God since I moved out.

I found myself in prayer, asking to be a great mom, requesting curses that possibly awaited my baby to be broke!

On that autumn morning, that closet became my prayer closet.

I paid close attention to my body.

Exciting days became frequent in my life! The bookstore was my new fun place to visit; I discovered what I coined my pregnancy bible, "What to Expect When you're Expecting," there! The book held answers to any question and experience pregnant women had broken down by each trimester!

Cliff gave me a hundred dollars to go grocery shop. I purchased what I was cooking, junk food for the most part, and Pepsi, not in bulk. My choice of items tickled him, which was understandable since it was my first-time grocery shopping for a family. Honestly, I had no idea what to get or how I would spend that much money at the store! Trista was the homemaker; I should've let her go to the store. Cooking the food was worse; the eggs I made for breakfast had small eggshell fragments.

New Yorkers and Southerners were like day and night. Talking behind folks' backs was and still is a popular southern tradition. Cliff made it known in your face when you were doing something that he didn't like; it hurt my feelings a little bit. That trip to the store taught me to make a list next time since we were playing house.

# NY Family

For the first time, I would be away from my family on the Thanksgiving holiday. I was a little nervous about flying pregnant and missing my favorite dishes, which no one could throw down in the kitchen like my family, so I thought, as Cliff told me, we were spending the holidays in NY.

The flight was great. The experience was completely different than my first trip.

The city moved at a fast pace, very FAST!! My eyes darted all over the place during the cab to his sisters.

Cliff's family was very nice. I braided his niece's hair, and we found out his sister and her husband were expecting around the same time as us!

Cliff repeatedly told me to stop looking up, an instinct very difficult to stop over a weekend around the tallest buildings in the world.

Cliff was a gracious host. My first time shopping in the Bronx was overwhelming narrowing down which store to enter. It was so unfair they had access to all the good stuff! From that day I forward I wanted every shoe and article of clothing I wore to come from New York!

We hung out at KD's apartment the night before Thanksgiving... the dude called me Monique, which was Cliff's ex-girlfriend! Was he serious or mad we were together? I didn't sweat it, I rolled my eyes and I fell asleep watching them play pool.

Thanksgiving morning, Cliff's sister was getting down in the kitchen; it smelled like Nan's. Everyone was dressed up! Cliff's niece had on a dress! I had a nice sweater and jeans; thank God I went shopping and could switch up my look. Down south and the north were so different. My accent stood out tremendously in New York.

Before we said the blessing, I inspected the food like I was Nan, pleasantly surprised at how delicious everything looked; the only thing missing was cranberry sauce; it wasn't Thanksgiving without it! I made Cliff aware, a little embarrassed, and he ran to get some.

They laughed about it, maybe because they thought I was craving it, but seriously, it was a must-have since I could remember.

When I called Nan's the noise in the background indicated there was a full house as usual. Of course, Uncle Ricardo and Aunt India's signature hearty "HEYYYYY" could be heard signaling to those in earshot to see who they were greeting.

Friday, we went to Cliff's older brother's place. It was nice meeting his wife and niece. Their spot was gorgeous in Co-Op City!

# Back to Reality

Back in N.C., I refused to be tucked away in the house; I was getting out this Saturday night! The weight looked good on me, especially from behind! I just looked like I gained the weight I always wanted. The stores in NY held endless fashions, and I was thrilled with my selections! I got two bubble coats; a fuchsia trimmed in black and a black patent leather one, which I planned to wear with all black. The black snakeskin patent leather boots set off the entire situation. I admired that I had all types of gear no one else could access.

Monday at the office, the new trainee class was now out on the floor taking calls. The verdict was still out so I held back the urge to be chipper with Jenifer, which was difficult because I'm usually friendly. Deception made me uncomfortable and not being myself made me feel unauthentic. My trust issues ran deep. Knowingly sharing men wasn't my style! I couldn't help but equate sex with their exchanges not a friend helping a friend. Growing up, "men are dogs" was said in my presence repeatedly. I like to give people the benefit of the doubt, so Cliff wasn't a dog, but I smelled a rat.

Cliff moved at a fast pace and had daily goals. I just wanted to lay in bed with him all day. Eventually, you become like the people you hang around. His plans were like no other man I'd encountered. I put some pep in my step and believed his dreams would come true and I'd be in attendance. Love, loyalty, steamy lust, and trust are what I offered. He was easy to love and be there for when he needed me in return. We were convenient to one another. Immature, pregnant, and broke, the arrangement worked for us both. I was his shelter; he made my house a home.

Knowing he had my back made me feel like a goddess!

The revelation from Cliff that I was the first girl to ever shed tears over him made me fill sorry him a little and I enforced my love even more. Love was the currency I gave freely. Cliff love language was to freely give money to those in his circle in need. I wanted to give and be a blessing some day and Break the ceiling of poverty over my families head.   The baby growing inside me was our new bond. I was thankful he cared and was present, despite voices in the background unaware of the sides of him I had experienced.

# Wholesome Dope Girl

Downtown, paying bills, I returned to my car with a boot on the tire. The ticket issuer directed me to this office after explaining the car had unpaid tickets.

Breaking the rules had caught up with me. Cliff paid the $1400 in the past due tickets. I don't know how I would've gotten the boot off if I didn't know him.

Cliff accompanied me to the sonogram, I was happy he was in town.

Unfortunately, I used the restroom before my name was called; the nurse had me drink the 32oz of water required to drink before the sonogram appointment again!

My sonogram didn't reveal the sex of the baby, but the doctor explained my child would be bigger and taller than me.

My bag for "delivery day," consisted of an outfit for a girl and a boy, although Cliff turned into a prophet and told me we were having a girl.

Pregnancy made me calm down, knowing stress affected the baby.

After Cliff was around for a while, souls behind the church mask were revealed. God sent a man from five hundred miles away to tell me, "Your family treats you like shit, and you don't deserve the treatment!" Funny, I came from stock focused on me being an unwed mother to an "unsaved" man. He came from stock concentrated on "what kind of family ignore molestation?"

I made decisions my family may not have agreed with, and rightfully so. They weren't footing any bills. No 18-year-old should ever have to move prematurely because their safety is at risk! I was happier than ever with all my decisions! New Yorkers road in cabs; in my little country city, it wasn't very cool to take a cab; it meant you could not afford it or did not have a car. Cliff could care less. I eventually taught him how to drive a straight drive; I wasn't going to transport myself to the hospital during labor. My pregnancy bible explained delivery could take place as early as 32 weeks. Nan would've had a fit if she knew I was teaching a man how to drive; she also would be disturbed that I was letting him drive my vehicle when he wasn't on my insurance, not knowing was paying my car insurance. If anything happened to the car, he could also get that fixed. Cliff caught on quickly in the vast Wake Forest Football Stadium lot.

Elevator chatter in the Reynolds Tower was high during the holidays; I gladly announced going to New York, when asked what my plans were as the elevator went down to the Lobby. Call me insecure still didn't know what the tea was. Cliff picked me up from work. He and Jenifer weren't friendly.

When "I" ran into my home girl's significant other, we were excited and even hugged sometimes when we saw each other; Cliff and Jenifer were distant and didn't acknowledge one another. Acting blind after what I'd been through growing up wasn't easy. Cliff wasn't just anybody; I was no longer a high schooler. Church mocked unwed church girls, but God in power and majesty granted this church girl with maturity to handle problems differently during the pregnancy. Being chill in the midst of chaos was my new mood. Getting upset and behaving petty had gotten old; chin lifted, I snapped out of it and pondered on what I wanted for dinner, soon Cliff would be asking me my favorite question he asked after work, "What do you want to eat?"

The child developing in my womb was my focus! December 31, 1995, came fast. I kept tradition and went to Atlanta to bring in the New Year in ATL at Club 112 with my girls Natalie and Money! I couldn't drink but being in The A was always a vibe! I felt the baby kick for the first time at the hotel the morning of 1/1/1996, New Year's Day. I was so ecstatic I called and told everyone!

# It's Spring Again

Spring was nearing. Cliff woke up apparently with the baby on his baby to come home to a new place with fresh paint, and I knew the perfect place! Excited, I got on the task immediately. Miss Creekway lived in these townhouses that I loved, located in a cute area that bordered the city called Old town. I had no life, so this task thrilled me. I was impressed with Cliff's thinking as I drove over to see if any townhouses were vacant! Luckily one was available. After speaking with someone at the number on the "For Rent" sign, I found out about the availability and monthly rent of the townhouse.

Cliff and I went to the leasing office to get the key and took a tour. We applied when we took the key back, and with my credit and his money, we got approved and moved in soon after!

I discovered the area thanks to my elementary school "day one!" I wasn't just moving I was becoming neighbors with Miss Creekway!!!! We didn't live side by side but I thank God I literally could exit my kitchen, take a few steps ahead and access her whenever I pleased!!!   I loved the cute suburbia feel the small city exuded and the fact my mail would no longer say Winston-Salem! I admired the area since she and Big Daddy relocated there.

My belly was getting huge! I dressed for comfort. Looks didn't matter. Green Espree slides were the only shoes that felt good on my swollen feet. Oversized T-shirts with tights became my couture of choice.

It was my first full-term pregnancy. I didn't know what to expect. I learned not to let anything or anyone stress me out, especially during pregnancy. My momma was hospitalized and diagnosed with toxemia when pregnant with my sister Emily. Nan said it was because Evan stressed her out during her pregnancy. I'd never let a man stress me out that I knew made my daughter uncomfortable, let alone bring a child into the world with him!

Looks and independence is what Cliff admired about me. I made survival mode look good, never looked at myself as independent or felt I had my shit together until he brought it to my attention. As quickly as he boosted my ego, it was deflated one morning after breakfast when he abruptly pulled over to the shoe store within walking distance from our new place and told me I needed new shoes! The edges of the heel of the shoe had worn down in his eyes; I loved sliding around in the shoes with the leaning heels, I was getting so big the worn out slides didn't embarrass me one iota! I got out of the car, and we went on in. Cliff suggested I get sneakers. The suggestion was GREAT, but he made me throw the green slides away after the purchase! You are not my daddy is what I wanted to tell him, as I walked out of the store like a kid wearing sneakers. Already grateful the man paid off my parking tickets, and I gave me the option to open a salon, I knew asking for a new pair of sneakers for every day of the week with thirty sweat suits to match was an option, but it was something I could get on my own. He had done so much already that I didn't want to be that girl!! Growing up, being told no, I didn't ask people for stuff or bother what wasn't mine. I prided myself on being trustworthy. I knew some chicks that would've spent his money and had other niggas on the side taking their money as well; that just was not me!

# Showers of Blessings

Paula hosted my baby shower!! LOL, I'll never forget the day I told her I was pregnant "you ain't have nothing better to do!" was her response. Paula was a jewel! She was my big sister from another mother. Although I met her in a business setting, Paula took me under her wing once I became her hairdresser. After the first invite to her house, I'd show up on weeknights and be there till almost bedtime. Hell, I was a teenager with a license; of all the places I could've been, this is where I wanted to be. The lessons I learned observing her care for Tate, my upbringing, and babysitting my sisters came in handy for parenting.

The shower was amazing!

Black has always been my favorite color, so naturally, black was the color of the two-piece bell-bottom ensemble I wore to the baby shower. The slinky material and wedges were not the safest option, but it was fashionable! My belly was enormous; the extra-large shirt fit fine. I needed a medium in the pants I had jacked up over my stomach to my bra. As I walked, I almost fell because they were too long. Paula saw me keep stepping on the pants a few times. I was sure she would soon say, "You going to break yo dam neck," but let me live on my special day. I was gone be cute if I fell!

The food was terrific and you know a Dewey's cake and cake squares were in the house. My friends showed up looking fabulous!! Cassidy had obliviously made a salon visit to my mentor and hairstylist Alexander; sis debuted a beautiful platinum natural close cut revealing her pretty c shape curls at the shower, her all mint green ensemble definitely screamed baby shower and complimented her well! I was so pleased with the crowd, they blessed me with so many gifts! We played games and laughed! Paula invited all of my "good Judies" together and even contacted clients she interacted with when she came for her hair appointments. I LOVE "Charlies Angels!!" Paula and Mia had outdone themselves!

When I arrived home, Cliff hadn't made it back from out of town, so I paged him!

Nan would've had a fit knowing I unloaded the car full of gifts alone, including two bassinets! I told him I enjoyed the shower and about all the gifts when he returned my call.

The day was so beautiful I refused to end it with a pity party as the spirit of loneliness greeted me at the door.

Waiting for Cliff to respond to sky pages gave me the creeps the closer we were to the baby's due date. Fear he would be out of town, not by my side, and miss the birth of his child altogether festered in my mind!

Sundays in the spring, I hung out at the park and lake. He was wherever he was; I was bored and pregnant, thinking about all the fun my friends were on the way to have at The Lake and High Point Park.

Shopping was therapeutic since I couldn't smoke to soothe myself. In mommy mode, I planned to go, baby shopping the next day.

# Getting To Know You, Getting to Know All About You

On maternity leave, I was able to enjoy the townhouse. It was fun at first. I stayed up late and woke up late.

Pregnant women had hangouts, when Miss Creekway was pregnant I tagged along with her to her favorite hangout, Walmart. The book store and baby section of Toys R Us became one of my favorite places to go! I purchased the Mercedes Benz of strollers; it was sleek and had three wheels instead of 4!

The baby's room was coming together; the bed was up with my waterbed from momma's house to lay on while the baby fell asleep. I frequented the room, often excited the baby was on the way! I had gone from an apartment with a hair room to a townhouse with a baby room.

My February night cravings for watermelon changed to a slice of pizza and grape jelly biscuits from scratch.

Cliff lounged and looked at basketball; sometimes our next door neighbor Glenn joined him; the two basketball fans balled at the park too. Cliff watched Colombo at 3pm whenever he was near a television.

After my nap, I watched Jerry Springer and Oprah in the living room.

Like magic, around six o'clock, Cliff would be like, "Ma, I'm hungry," or ask, "what are you going to feed my daughter?"

We enjoyed grilling with Miss Creekway and Big Daddy and they turned us on to this Japanese restaurant Kyoto that became our favorite restaurant. Aside from the prom this was the most expensive meal I had eaten just because it was dinner time and loving it!. Uncle Miles owned a black three series BMW that I adored and since I had a coupe I was lovey to be driven in Big Daddy and Miss Creekway spacious powder blue five series!

# Motherhood

Telepathic thoughts from humans could be felt all over Earth, mine must've reached Teeka in ATL! She called and was the perfect person to express how ready for labor and exhausted I was. Glad I brought it up because she had a remedy for me, and since she already gave birth to a child, I trusted her judgment.

The situation required a trip to the ABC Store/bar and the Drugstore. I got dressed and decided my best bet was Hanes Mall since the drugstore and a bar were there. I cringed at being watched to the car after leaving the bar, so I parked at the Eckerd Drugs

Entrance. The sales clerk helped me locate the castor oil. Annabelle's was empty; I sat in the back of the restaurant near the restroom. The waitress raised a brow when I placed the order with my big stomach; she brought the shot of liquor to me anyway. Silverware, shot, and castor oil prepped; I took the drink, then a spoonful of castor oil, and left. I wasn't drunk, and I wasn't going to tell Cliff about that restaurant visit.

I don't know which was worse, the cocktail or eating Ajax the last trimester. Traces of comet residue were in my car console, similar to the cornstarch on momma's housecoat. Being Anemic caused her to crave cornstarch like I craved Ajax. I kept a plastic bag full of Ajax or Comet on me at all times. I'd wet my index finger, stick it in the Ajax, then relish it like cake icing due to an iron deficiency. The 1-800 number Comet rep, with no judgment, explained I'd be okay because the cleaner exited out the body through the bowels if swallowed. The rest of the day, I waited for the remedy to kick in.

We watched television and ate Famous Amos cookies with pecans like any other night and got in bed at 1 a.m.

Not long after Cliff and I laid down, I felt a warm liquid come out of me; it was faint pastel pink on the tissue. I woke Cliff up and turned on the light. We pulled back the bedspread, and the same pale pink was on the white sheets. I phoned the doctor, and he told me to go to the hospital. It was raining. Cliff's driving was rough as he changed gears; I could feel every jerk.

After our safe arrival and being admitted, according to the triage nurse, I was 4 centimeters.

The epidural needle was all I could think about once I finally reached the day of delivery. Fixated on the machine that monitored my contractions, I discovered it shows you the contraction before it came, so I stopped watching it, terrorized by the warnings!

Things moved along once momma arrived. Emily and Brooklyn were grinning and peeking in through the window in the door just like I did when Emily was born. Cliff was reading the newspaper as my contractions worsened, I could feel pain, but luckily I was shaking too much to get the dreadful epidural shot! It was a no for me when friends with children told me how long the needle was.

The pain medicine in my IV relaxed me; I was wide awake when it was time for my legs to go in the stir-ups; my legs gapped open so wide a woman lost all dignity!

"Do something Cliff!" I heard my momma plead, and he grabbed my hand. I held on tight and braced myself to push, and on the last push, as if I was coming up on a big hill in the last seat of a roller coaster speeding downhill, at 10:28 am 5/28/96, our daughter arrived Memorial Day week!

The second day after the delivery, I was up moving around the hospital. The baby was more beautiful than I could imagine. Her red birthmark above her lip had a circular shape like a pizza with sauce minus the cheese. God had a sense of humor because that's all I mainly ate while I was pregnant. I was so glad she didn't have a long narrow face like mine I got picked on so horribly for growing up.

Cliff told me he had a different respect for nurses. According to him, while I was doped up liquids were coming from every exit on my body without hesitation; they rescued me in pretty gross moments!

The day I left the hospital, I was informed I had an appointment with WIC, so we had a pit stop on the way home. I was surprised it was made the same day I left the hospital. Nan would've demanded the appointment date be after I heal and the baby's six-week check-up.

Cliff pushed us to the car in the wheelchair the hospital provided, and we made the pit stop. I hadn't used my legs much. I couldn't imagine driving a straight drive or carrying the baby to the appointment. Thank God her father was present to watch her in the car and our fresh newborn wasn't exposed to germs.

I was sore from the delivery and entered the building walking like a cowgirl.

A lady spoke with me briefly and informed me about the WIC Program, which offered healthy food options for the baby and family. They gave me Enfamil formula and took me to a room full of non-perishable foods to select items. WIC would mail a voucher monthly after that visit. I was very grateful for the appointment and all the money I'd save not purchasing baby milk.

I was a smoker but the hospital made me give them the side-eye because feeding the baby naturally with breastmilk wasn't recommended or mentioned to "us." Asking new moms to breastfeed rather than setting up an appointment must've been customary. Regardless of my decision to bottle feed it was an offensive practice. Prioritizing getting back to my Newport's was a young and selfish decision being aware of the nutrients the mother provided through breastmilk, to even the slave masters wife's newborns on plantations.

# Home Sweet Home

Cliff had the aromatherapy going with my favorite candles. He changed the theme of the baby room to Winnie the Pooh, which was excellent.

Normal clothes awaited me, I headed to my closet after taking it all in the fact I brought a whole human home with me from the hospital and attempted to try on clothes that wouldn't budge past my thigh!

1995 no one could've told me I'd be a mother in 1996. I now had the opportunity to care for someone how I deemed fit; my daughter's life would be different. I would protect her and vowed I would be single if her father and I broke up, a STEPFATHER would not be in her future.

# Ecclesiastes:

Churches require premarital counseling for candidates of marriage, some candidates must profess their faith before the session is solidified. The session supposedly deepens relationships. Candidates must profess their faith before the pastor will conduct the ceremony. Discussions of intimacy, money matters, and the importance of communication and how to divide chores is had but not one session physically includes pre-existing children involved in the future Union.

Post ceremony is all about the newlyweds, but what about the kids?

First Thessalonians 5:17

Pray without ceasing

THANK YOU READING!!

I hope you enjoyed the book and gained clues and resolutions to rescue children being abused in any form in your village.

A lady emerges, leaving the church girl in the dust but tucked deep in her heart.

Register on the email list:

ladylikechurchgirl2023@gmail.com

In celebration of my birthday and a special thanks to readers, get a sneak peek of the intro to the next (untitled) book 4/2/23!

Made in the USA
Columbia, SC
25 March 2024

33569597R00130